The Best of the World's Classics

VOL. IX

AMERICA—I

1579—1891

THE BEST OF THE WORLD'S CLASSICS

RESTRICTED TO PROSE

HENRY CABOT LODGE
EDITOR-IN-CHIEF

FRANCIS W. HALSEY
ASSOCIATE EDITOR

With an Introduction, Biographical and Explanatory Notes, etc.

IN TEN VOLUMES

Vol. IX
AMERICA—I

FUNK & WAGNALLS COMPANY
NEW YORK AND LONDON

COPYRIGHT, 1909, BY
FUNK & WAGNALLS COMPANY
[*Printed in the United States of America*]

CONTENTS

Vol. IX—America—I

	Page
JOHN SMITH—(Born in 1579, died in 1631.)	
His Story of Pocahontas. (From the "General History of Virginia")	3
WILLIAM BRADFORD—(Born in 1590, died in 1657.)	
The Pilgrims Land and Meet the Indians. (From the "History of Plymouth")	11
SAMUEL SEWALL—(Born in 1652, died in 1730.)	
How He Courted Madam Winthrop. (From his "Diary")	19
COTTON MATHER—(Born in 1663, died in 1728.)	
In Praise of John Eliot. (From the "Magnalia Christi Americana")	33
WILLIAM BYRD—(Born in 1674, died in 1744.)	
At the Home of Colonel Spotswood. (From "A Visit to the Mines")	38
JONATHAN EDWARDS—(Born in 1703, died in 1758.)	
Of Liberty and Moral Agencies. (From the "Freedom of the Will")	44
BENJAMIN FRANKLIN—(Born in 1706, died in 1790.)	
I His First Entry into Philadelphia. (From the "Autobiography")	51

CONTENTS

	Page
II Warnings Braddock Did Not Heed. (From the "Autobiography")	55
III How to Draw Lightning from the Clouds. (From a letter to Peter Collinson)	59
IV The Way to Wealth. (From "Poor Richard's Almanac")	61
V Dialog with the Gout	68
VI A Proposal to Madame Helvetius. (A letter to Madame Helvetius)	76

GEORGE WASHINGTON—(Born in 1732, died in 1799.)

I To His Wife on Taking Command of the Army. (A letter written on June 18, 1775)	79
II Of His Army in Cambridge. (A letter to Joseph Reed)	81
III To the Marquis Chastellux on His Marriage. (A letter of April 25, 1788)	84

JOHN ADAMS—(Born in 1735, died in 1826.)

I On His Nomination of Washington to Be Commander-in-Chief. (From his "Diary")	87
II An Estimate of Franklin. (From a letter to the Boston *Patriot*)	90

THOMAS PAINE — Born in 1737, died in 1809.)

In Favor of the Separation of the Colonies from Great Britain. (From "Common Sense")	94

THOMAS JEFFERSON—(Born in 1743, died in 1826.)

I When the Bastile Fell. (From his "Autobiography")	98

CONTENTS

	Page
II The Futility of Disputes. (From a letter to his nephew)	106
III Of Blacks and Whites in the South. (From the "Notes on the State of Virginia")	108
IV His Account of Logan's Famous Speech. (From the "Notes on Virginia")	114

GOUVERNEUR MORRIS—(Born in 1752, died in 1816.)

I The Opening of the French States-General. (From a letter to Mrs. Morris)	117
II Of the Execution of Louis XVI. (From a letter to Thomas Jefferson)	120

ALEXANDER HAMILTON—(Born in 1757, died in 1804.)

I Of the Failure of Confederation. (From *The Federalist*)	123
II His Reasons for not Declining Burr's Challenge. (From a statement written before the day of the duel)	129

JOHN QUINCY ADAMS—(Born in 1767, died in 1848.)

I Of His Mother. (From the "Diary")	133
II The Moral Taint Inherent in Slavery. (From the "Diary")	135

WILLIAM E. CHANNING—(Born in 1780, died in 1842.)

Of Greatness in Napoleon. (From a review of Scott's "Life of Napoleon")	139

CONTENTS

		Page
John James Audubon—(Born in 1780, died in 1857.)		
	Where the Mocking Bird Dwells. (From the "Birds of America")	144
Washington Irving—(Born in 1783, died in 1859.)		
	I The Last of the Dutch Governors of New York. (From "Knickerbocker's History of New York")	147
	II The Awakening of Rip Van Winkle. (From the "Sketch Book")	151
	III At Abbotsford with Scott. (From the "Crayon Miscellany")	161
Fenimore Cooper—(Born in 1789, died in 1851.)		
	I His Father's Arrival at Otsego Lake. (From "The Pioneers")	170
	II Running the Gantlet. (From "The Last of the Mohicans")	178
	III Leather-Stocking's Farewell. (From "The Pioneers")	185
William Cullen Bryant—(Born in 1794, died in 1878.)		
	An October Day in Florence. (From a letter)	194
William H. Prescott—(Born in 1796, died in 1859.)		
	I The Fate of Egmont and Hoorne. (From "Philip II")	198
	II The Genesis of Don Quixote. (From the "Miscellanies")	209

CONTENTS

	Page
GEORGE BANCROFT—(Born in 1800, died in 1891.)	
The Fate of Evangeline's Countrymen. (From the "History of the United States")	217
RALPH WALDO EMERSON—(Born in 1803, died in 1882.)	
I Thoreau's Broken Task. (From the "Funeral Address")	223
II The Intellectual Honesty of Montaigne. (From "Representative Men")	229
III His Visit to Carlyle at Craigenputtock. (From "English Traits")	231
NATHANIEL HAWTHORNE—(Born in 1804, died in 1864.)	
I Occupants of an Old Manse. (From "Mosses from an Old Manse")	235
II Arthur Dimmesdale on the Scaffold. (From "The Scarlet Letter")	242
III Of Life at Brook Farm. (From "The Blithedale Romance")	248
IV The Death of Judge Pyncheon. (From "The House of the Seven Gables")	252

AMERICA—I

1579—1891

JOHN SMITH

Born in England in 1579, died in 1631; served against the Turks, captured, but escaped and returned to England in 1605; sailed for Virginia in 1606, and helped to found Jamestown; captured by Indians and his life saved by Pocahontas the same year; explored the Chesapeake to its head; president of the Colony in 1608; returned to London in 1609; in 1614 explored the coast of New England; captured by the French in 1615 and escaped the same year; received the title of Admiral of New England in 1617; published his "True Relation" in 1608, "Map of Virginia" in 1612, "A Description of New England" in 1616, "New England's Trials" in 1620, and his "General History" in 1624.

HIS STORY OF POCAHONTAS[1]

HERE more than two hundred of those grim Courtiers stood wondering at him [John Smith], as he had beene a monster; till Powhatan[2] and his train had put themselves in their greatest braveries. Before a fire upon a seat like a bedsted, he sat covered with a great robe, made of Rarowcun skinnes, and all the tayles hanging by. On either hand did sit a young wench of 16 or 18 years, and along on each side the house, two rowes of men, and behind them as many women, with all their heads

[1] From Smith's "Generall Historie of Virginia."

[2] Powhatan was chief of a confederacy of Indians known as the Powhatans, which he had raised from one comprizing only seven tribes to one of thirty. The word Powhatan means "falls in a stream," and was originally applied to the falls in the James river at Richmond.

and shoulders painted red; many of their heads bedecked with the white downe of Birds; but every one with something: and a great chain of white beads about their necks.

At his entrance before the King, all the people gave a great shout. The Queene of Appamatuck was appointed to bring him water to wash his hands, and another brought him a bunch of feathers, instead of a towel to dry them. Having feasted him after their best barbarous manner they could, a long consultation was held, but the conclusion was, two great stones were brought before Powhatan: then as many as could laid hands on him, dragged him to them, and thereon laid his head, and being ready with their clubs, to beate out his braines, Pocahontas the King's dearest daughter, when no intreaty could prevaile, got his head in her armes, and laid her owne upon his to save him from death: whereat the Emperour was contented he should live to make him hatchets, and her bells, beads, and copper; for they thought him as well of all occupations as themselves. For the King himselfe will make his owne robes, shooes, bowes, arrowes, pots; plant, hunt, or doe any thing so well as the rest. . . .

To conclude our peace, thus it happened. Captaine Argall[3] having entered into a great acquaintance with Japazaws, an old friend of Captaine Smith's, and so to all our Nation, ever since hee discovered the Countrie: hard by him

[3] Argall, through intimidation or bribery, had made Pocahontas a captive in 1612, when she was the wife of an Indian attached to her father as a subordinate chief or leader.

JOHN SMITH

there was Pocahontas, whom Captaine Smith's Relations intituleth the Numparell of Virginia, and tho she had beene many times a preserver of him and the whole Colonie, yet till this accident shee was never seene at James towne since his departure, being at Patawomeke, as it seemes, thinking her selfe unknown, was easily by her friend Japazaws perswaded to goe abroad with him and his wife to see the ship, for Captaine Argall had promised him a Copper Kettle to bring her but to him, promising no way to hurt her, but keepe her till they could conclude a peace with her father. The Salvage for this Copper Kettle would have done any thing, it seemed by the Relation; for tho she had seene and beene in many ships, yet he caused his wife to faine how desirous she was to see one, and that he offered to beat her for her importunitie, till she wept.

But at last he told her, if Pocahontas would goe with her, he was content: and thus they betrayed the poore innocent Pocahontas aboord, where they were all kindly feasted in the cabin. Japazaws treading oft on the Captaine's foot, to remember he had done his part, the Captaine when he saw his time, perswaded Pocahontas to the gun-roome, faining to have some conference with Japazaws, which was only that she should not perceive he was any way guiltie of her captivitie: so sending for her againe, he told her before her friends, she must goe with him, and compound peace betwixt her Countrie and us, before she ever should see Powhatan, whereat the old Jew and his wife began to howle and crie as fast as Pocahontas, that upon the Captaine's fair perswasions, by degrees pacifying her selfe, and Japazaws and his wife, with the Kettle and other toys, went merrily on shore, and she to James towne. A messenger forthwith was sent to her father, that his daughter Pocahontas he loved so dearly, he must ransome with our men, swords, pieces, tooles, etc., he trecherously had stolne. . . .

Long before this, Master John Rolfe, an honest Gentleman, and of good behaviour, had beene in love with Pocahontas, and she with him, which thing at that instant I made knowne to Sir Thomas Dale by a letter from him, wherein hee intreated his advice, and she acquainted her brother with it, which resolution Sir Thomas Dale [4] well approved. The bruit of this mariage came soone to the knowledge of Powhatan, a thing acceptable to him, as appeared by his sudden consent, for within ten days he sent Opachisco, an old Uncle of hers, and two of his sons, to see the manner of the mariage, and to doe in that behalfe what they requested, for the confirmation thereof, as his deputie; which was accordingly done about the first of Aprill. And ever since we have had friendly trade and commerce, as well with Powhatan himself, as all his subjects. . . .

The Lady Rebecca,[5] alias Pocahontas, daughter to Powhattan, by the diligent care of Master John Rolfe her husband and his friends, as taught to

[4] Dale was colonial governor of Virginia in 1611 and again in 1614-16. In the latter year he returned to England, taking with him Captain Rolfe and Pocahontas.

[5] Under that name Pocahontas had been baptized in the original Jamestown church. A legend has survived that an old font, now preserved in the church at Williamsburg, is the one from which she was baptized.

JOHN SMITH

speake such English as might well bee understood, well instructed in Christianitie, and was become very formal and civil after our English manner; she had also by him a childe which she loved most dearely and the Treasurer and Company tooke order both for the maintenance of her and it, besides there were divers persons of great ranke and qualitie had beene very kinde to her; and before she arrived at London, Captaine Smith to deserve her former courtesies, made her qualities knowne to the Queene's most excellent Majestie and her Court, and writ a little booke to this effect to the Queene: An abstract whereof followeth.

"*To the most high and vertuous Princesse Queene Anne of Great Brittanie.*

"MOST ADMIRED QUEENE,

"The love I beare my God, my King, and Countrie hath so oft emboldened me in the worst of extreme dangers, that now honestie doth constraine mee presume thus far beyond my selfe, to present your Majestie this short discourse: If ingratitude be a deadly poyson to all honest vertues, I must bee guiltie of that crime if I should omit any meanes to bee thankful. So it is, that some ten yeers agoe being in Virginia, and taken prisoner by the power of Powhatan their chiefe King, I received from this great Salvage exceeding great courtesie, especially from his son Nantaquaus, the most manliest, comeliest, boldest spirit, I ever saw in a Salvage, and his sister Pocahontas, the King's most deare and well-beloved daughter, being but a childe of twelve or thirteene yeers of age, whose compassionate pitiful heart, of desperate estate, gave me much cause to respect her: I being the first Christian this proud King and his grim attendants ever saw: and thus inthralled in their barbarous power, I cannot say I felt the least occasion of want that was in the power of those my mortal foes to prevent, notwithstanding all their threats. After some six weeks fatting among those Salvage Courtiers, at the minute of my execution, she hazarded the beating out of her owne braines to save mine, and not only that, but so prevaild with her father, that I was safely conducted to James towne, where I found about eight and thirtie miserable poore and sicke creatures, to keepe possession of all those large territories of Virginia. Such was the weaknesse of this poore Commonwealth, as had the Salvages not fed us, we directly had starved.

"And this reliefe, most gracious Queene, was commonly brought us by this Lady Pocahontas, notwithstanding all these passages when inconstant Fortune turned our peace to war, this tender Virgin would still not spare to dare to visit us, and by her our jars have beene oft appeased, and our wants still supplyed; were it the policie of her father thus to imploy her, or the ordinance of God thus to make her His instrument, or her extraordinary affection to our Nation, I know not: but of this I am sure:—when her father with the utmost of his policie and power, sought to surprize mee, having but eighteene with mee, the darke night could not affright her from comming through the irkesome woods, and with watered eyes gave me intelligence, with her best advice to escape his furie; which had hee knowne, hee had surely slaine her. James towne with her

JOHN SMITH

wild traine she as freely frequented, as her father's habitation; and during the time of two or three yeeres, she next under God, was still the instrument to preserve this Colonie from death, famine and utter confusion, which if in those times had once beene dissolved, Virginia might have line as it was at our first arrival to this day. Since then, this businesse having beene turned and varied by many accidents from that I left it at: it is most certaine, after a long and troublesome war after my departure, betwixt her father and our Colonie, all which time shee was not heard of, about two yeeres after she her selfe was taken prisoner, being so detained neere two yeeres longer, the Colonie by that meanes was relieved, peace concluded, and at last rejecting her barbarous condition, was maried to an English Gentleman, with whom at this present she is in England; the first Christian ever of that Nation, the first Virginian ever spake English, or had a childe in mariage by an Englishman, a matter surely, if my meaning bee truly considered and well understood, worthy a Prince's understanding. . . .

The small time I staid in London, divers Courtiers and others, my acquaintances, hath gone with mee to see her, that generally concluded, they did thinke God had a great hand in her conversion, and they have seen many English Ladies worse favored, proportioned and behaviored, and as since I have heard, it pleased both the King and Queene's Majestie honorably to esteeme her, accompanied with that honorable Lady the Lady De la Warre, and that honorable Lord her husband, and divers other persons of good qualities, both publikely at the maskes and otherwise, to her great satisfaction and content, which doubtlesse she would have deserved had she lived to arrive in Virginia.[6]

[6] Pocahontas in England gave birth to a son. She died at Gravesend in the following year, in 1617. The parish records of Gravesend describe her as "a Virginia lady borne, here was buried in ye chauncell." In London a well-known street preserves a memorial of her in its name—La Belle Sauvage. Her son, Thomas Rolfe, after living many years in England, settled in Virginia. Several families in that State have traced their descent from him. One of these was the famous John Randolph of Roanoke.

WILLIAM BRADFORD

Born in England in 1590, died at Plymouth, Mass., in 1657; governor of Plymouth Colony from 1627, except for five years, to 1657; wrote a "History of the Plymouth Plantation" for the period 1602-47, the manuscript of which was lost in England, but after the lapse of about seventy-five years it was found in a library in 1855, and in the following year published.

THE PILGRIMS LAND AND MEET THE INDIANS[1]
(1620)

HAVING the wind good, we sailed all that day along the coast about fifteen leagues; but saw neither river nor creek to put into. After we had sailed an hour or two, it began to snow and rain, and to be bad weather. About the midst of the afternoon the wind increased, and the seas began to be very rough; and the hinges of the rudder broke, so that we could steer no longer with it, but two men, with much ado, were fain to serve with a couple of oars. The seas were grown so great that we were much troubled and in great danger; and night grew on. Anon, Master Coppin bade us be of good cheer; he saw the harbor. As we drew near, the gale being

---

[1] From what was long known as "Mourt's Relation," published in London in 1622, but more properly, and now generally, called the "Journal," or diary, of Bradford and Edward Winslow. This important historical document covers the first year of the Plymouth colony.

stiff, and we bearing great sail to get in, split our mast in three pieces, and were like to have cast away our shallop. Yet, by God's mercy, recovering ourselves, we had the flood with us, and struck into the harbor.

Now he that thought that had been the place, was deceived, it being a place where not any of us had been before; and coming into the harbor, he that was our pilot, did bear up northward, which if he had continued, we had been cast away. Yet still the Lord kept us and we bare up for an island before us, and recovering of that island, being compassed about with many rocks, and dark night growing upon us, it pleased the Divine Providence that we fell upon a place of sandy ground, where our shallop did ride safe and secure all that night; and coming upon a strange island, kept our watch all night in the rain upon that island. And in the morning we marched about it, and found no inhabitants at all; and here we made our rendezvous all that day, being Saturday, 10th of December. On the Sabbath day we rested; and on Monday we sounded the harbor, and found it a very good harbor for our shipping. We marched also into the land, and found divers cornfields, and little running brooks, a place very good for situation. So we returned to our ship again with good news to the rest of our people, which did much comfort their hearts. . . .

Some of us, having a good mind, for safety, to plant in the greater isle, we crossed the bay, which is there five or six miles over, and found the isle about a mile and half or two miles about, all wooded, and no fresh water but two or three pits, that we doubted of fresh water in summer, and so full of wood as we could hardly clear so much as to serve us for corn. Besides, we judged it cold for our corn, and some part very rocky; yet divers thought of it as a place defensible, and of great security. That night we returned again a shipboard, with resolution the next morning to settle on some of those places.

So in the morning, after we had called on God for direction, we came to this resolution, to go presently ashore again, and to take a better view of two places which we thought most fitting for us; for we could not now take time for further search or consideration, our victuals being much spent, especially our beer, and it being now the 19th of December. After our landing and viewing of the places, so well as we could, we came to a conclusion, by most voices, to set on the main land, on the first place, on a high ground, where there is a great deal of land cleared, and hath been planted with corn three or four years ago; and there is a very sweet brook runs under the hill side, and many delicate springs of as good water as can be drunk, and where we may harbor our shallops and boats exceeding well; and in this brook much good fish in their seasons; on the further side of the river also much corn-ground cleared. In one field is a great hill, on which we point to make a platform, and plant our ordnance, which will command all round about. From thence we may see into the bay, and far into the sea; and we may see thence Cape Cod. Our greatest labor will be fetching of our wood, which is half a quarter of an English mile; but there is enough so far off. What people inhabit here we yet know not, for as yet we have seen none. So there we made our rendezvous, and a place for some of our people, about twenty, resolving in the morning to come all ashore and to build houses.

But the next morning, being Thursday, the 21st of December, it was stormy and wet, that we could not go ashore; and those that remained there all night could do nothing, but were wet, not having daylight enough to make them a sufficient court of guard, to keep them dry. All that night it blew and rained extremely. It was so tempestuous that the shallop could not go on land so soon as was meet, for they had no victuals on land. About eleven o'clock the shallop went off with much ado with provision, but could not return, it blew so strong; and was such foul weather that we were forced to let fall our anchor, and ride with three anchors ahead.

Friday, the 22d, the storm still continued, that we could not get a land, nor they come to us aboard. . . .

Saturday, the 23d, so many of us as could went on shore, felled and carried timber, to provide themselves stuff for building.

Sunday, the 24th, our people on shore heard a cry of some savages, as they thought, which caused an alarm and to stand on their guard, expecting an assault; but all was quiet.

Friday, the 16th, a fair warm day toward. This morning we determined to conclude of the military orders, which we had begun to consider of before, but were interrupted by the savages, as we mentioned formerly. And while we were busied, hereabout, we were interrupted again;

for there presented himself a savage, which caused an alarm. He very boldly came all alone, and along the houses, straight to the rendezvous; where we intercepted him, not suffering him to go in, as undoubtedly he would out of his boldness. He saluted us in English, and bade us "Welcome!" for he had learned some broken English among the Englishmen that came to fish at Monhiggon, and knew by name the most of the captains, commanders and masters, that usually come. He was a man free in speech, so far as he could express his mind, and of a seemly carriage. We questioned him of many things; he was the first savage we could meet withal. He said he was not of these parts, but of Morattiggon, and one of the sagamores or lords thereof; and had been eight months in these parts, it lying hence a day's sail with a great wind, and five days by land. He discoursed of the whole country, and of every province, and of their sagamores, and their number of men and strength. The wind beginning to rise a little, we cast a horseman's coat about him; for he was stark naked, only a leather about his waist, with a fringe about a span long or little more. He had a bow and two arrows, the one headed, and the other unheaded. He was a tall, straight man, the hair of his head black, long behind, only short before, none on his face at all. He asked some beer, but we gave him strong water, and biscuit, and butter, and cheese, and pudding, and a piece of mallard; all which he liked well, and had been acquainted with such amongst the English. He told us the place where we now live is called Patuxet, and that about four years ago all the inhabitants died of an extraordinary plague, and there is neither man, woman, nor child remaining, as indeed we have found none; so as there is none to hinder our possession, or to lay claim unto it. All the afternoon we spent in communication with him. We would gladly have been rid of him at night, but he was not willing to go this night. Then we thought to carry him on shipboard, wherewith he was well content, and went into the shallop; but the wind was high and the water scant, that it could not return back. We lodged him that night at Steven Hopkin's house, and watched him.

The next day he went away back to the Masasoits, from whence he said he came, who are our next bordering neighbors. They are sixty strong, as he saith. The Nausites are as near, southeast of them, and are a hundred strong; and those were they of whom our people were encountered, as we before related. They are much incensed and provoked against the English; and about eight months ago slew three Englishmen, and two more hardly escaped by flight to Monhiggon. They were Sir Ferdinando Gorge's[2] men, as this savage told us; as he did likewise of the *huggery*, that is, fight, that our discoverers had with the Nausites, and of our tools that were taken out of the woods, which we willed him, should be brought again; otherwise we would

---

[2] Gorge was an English naval and military commander who came of an ancient family in Somersetshire. He had undertaken several schemes of discovery and settlement in America, but with small success. His pioneer work, however, was of such importance that he has sometimes been called "the father of English colonization in America."

right ourselves. These people are ill affected toward the English by reason of one Hunt, a master of a ship, who deceived the people and got them, under color of trucking with them, twenty out of this very place where we inhabit, and seven men from the Nausites, and carried them away, and sold them for slaves, like a wretched man (for twenty pound a man) that cares not what mischief he doth for his profit.

Saturday, in the morning, we dismissed the savage, and gave him a knife, a bracelet, and a ring. He promised within a night or two to come again and to bring with him some of the Masasoits, our neighbors, with such beavers' skins as they had to truck with us.

Saturday and Sunday reasonable fair days. On this day came again the savage, and brought with him five other tall, proper men. They had every man a deer's skin on him, and the principal of them had a wild cat's skin, or such like, on the one arm. They had most of them long hosen up to their groins, close made, and above their groins to their waist another leather; they were altogether like the Irish trousers. They are of complexion like our English gipseys; no hair or very little on their faces; on their heads long hair to their shoulders, only cut before; some trussed up before with a feather, broad-wise, like a fan; another a fox-tail, hanging out. These left (according to our charge given him before) their bows and arrows a quarter of a mile from our town. We gave them entertainment as we thought was fitting them. They did eat liberally of our English victuals. They made semblance unto us of friendship and amity. They sang and danced after their manner, like antics. They brought with them in a thing like a bow-case (which the principal of them had about his waist) a little of their corn pounded to powder, which, put to a little water, they eat. He had a little tobacco in a bag; but none of them drank but when he liked. Some of them had their faces painted black, from the forehead to the chin, four or five fingers broad; others after other fashions, as they liked. They brought three or four skins; but we would not truck with them at all that day, but wished them to bring more, and we would truck for all; which they promised within a night or two, and would leave these behind them, tho we were not willing they should; and they brought us all our tools again, which were taken in the woods, in our men's absence. So, because of the day, we dismissed them so soon as we could. But Samoset,[3] our first acquaintance, either was sick or feigned himself so, and would not go with them, and stayed with us till Wednesday morning. Then we sent him to them to know the reason they came not according to their words; and we gave him a hat, a pair of stockings and shoes, a shirt, and a piece of cloth to tie about his waist.

[3] Samoset is still famous as an Indian who remained firm in his friendship with the Plymouth colonists.

SAMUEL SEWALL

Born in England in 1652, died in Boston in 1730; served in the Bay Colony as judge and in other public stations; one of the judges at trials for witchcraft in 1692; chief justice in 1718; a philanthropist, and in 1700 wrote a pamphlet against slavery; his other works: "Queries Respecting America," published in 1690; "The Kennebec Indians" in 1721, and his "Diary" covering the period 1664-1729 in 1882.

HOW HE COURTED MADAM WINTHROP[1]
(1720)

SEPTEMBER 5, 1720. Mary Hirst goes to Board with Madam Oliver and her Mother Loyd. Going to Son Sewall's I there meet with Madam Winthrop, told her I was glad to meet her there, had not seen her a great while; gave her Mr. Homes's Sermon. . . .

[1] From Sewall's "Diary," as published by the Massachusetts Historical Society in 1882.

Mrs. Winthrop was the widow of General Waite Still Winthrop, a son of John Winthrop, Governor of Connecticut, who was a son of John Winthrop, Governor of the Massachusetts Bay Colony. Her maiden name was Katharine Brattle. She had first married John Eyre, with whom she lived about twenty years, and by whom she had twelve children. She was born in 1664, and at the time of Sewall's courtship of her was fifty-six and he sixty-nine. General Winthrop and Mrs. Sewall had died a few years before within a month of each other. Madam Winthrop did not marry Judge Sewall, nor any one else. She died five years after the date of this courtship.

September 30. Mr. Colman's Lecture: Daughter Sewall acquaints Madam Winthrop that if she pleas'd to be within at 3 P.M. I would wait on her. She answer'd she would be at home.

October 1. Satterday, I dine at Mr. Stoddard's: from thence I went to Madam Winthrop's just at 3. Spake to her, saying, my loving wife died so soon and suddenly, 'twas hardly convenient for me to think of marrying again; however I came to this Resolution, that I would not make my Court to any person without first Consulting with her. Had a pleasant discourse about 7 [seven] Single persons sitting in the Fore-seat. She propounded one and another for me; but none would do, said Mrs. Loyd was about her Age.

October 3. 2. Waited on Madam Winthrop again; 'twas a little while before she came in. Her daughter Noyes being there alone with me, I said, I hoped my Waiting on her Mother would not be disagreeable to her. She answer'd she should not be against that that might be for her Comfort. I Saluted her, and told her I perceived I must shortly wish her a good Time; (her mother had told me, she was with Child, and within a Moneth or two of her Time). By and by in came Mr. Airs, Chaplain of the Castle, and hang'd up his Hat, which I was a little startled at, it seeming as if he was to lodge there. At last Madam Winthrop came too. After a considerable time, I went up to her and said, if it might not be inconvenient I desired to speak with her. She assented, and spake of going into another Room; but Mr. Airs and Mrs. Noyes presently rose up, and went out, leaving us there alone.

Then I usher'd in Discourse from the names in the Fore-seat; at last I pray'd that Katharine [Mrs. Winthrop] might be the person assign'd for me. She instantly took it up in the way of Denyal, as if she had catch'd at an Opportunity to do it, saying she could not do it before she was asked. Said that was her mind unless she should Change it, which she believed she should not; could not leave her Children. I express'd my Sorrow that she should do it so Speedily, pray'd her Consideration, and ask'd her when I should wait on her agen. She setting no time, I mentioned that day Sennight. Gave her Mr. Willard's Fountain open'd with the little print and verses; saying, I hop'd if we did well read that book, we should meet together hereafter, if we did not now. She took the Book, and put it in her Pocket. Took Leave.

October 5. Midweek, I din'ed with the Court; from thence went and visited Cousin Jonathan's wife, Lying in with her little Betty. Gave the Nurse 2s. Altho I had appointed to wait upon her, Madam Winthrop, next Monday, yet I went from my Cousin Sewall's thither about 3 P.M. The Nurse told me Madam dined abroad at her daughter Noyes's, they were to go out together. I ask'd for the Maid, who was not within. Gave Katee a penny and a Kiss, and came away. Accompanyed my Son and daughter Cooper in their Remove to their New House.

October 6. A little after 6 P.M. I went to Madam Winthrop's. She was not within. I gave Sarah Chickering the Maid 2s., Juno, who brought in wood, 1s. Afterward the Nurse came in, I gave her 18d., having no other small Bill.

After awhile Dr. Noyes came in with his Mother; and quickly after his wife came in: They sat talking, I think, till eight a-clock. I said I fear'd I might be some Interruption to their Business: Dr. Noyes reply'd pleasantly: He fear'd they might be an Interruption to me, and went away. Madam seem'd to harp upon the same string. Must take care of her Children; could not leave that House and Neighborhood where she had dwelt so long. I told her she might doe her children as much or more good by bestowing what she laid out in Hous-keeping, upon them. Said her Son would be of age the 7th of August. I said it might be inconvenient for her to dwell with her Daughter-in-Law, who must be Mistress of the House. I gave her a piece of Mr. Belcher's Cake and Ginger-Bread wrapped up in a clean sheet of Paper; told her of her Father's kindness to me when Treasurer, and I Constable. My Daughter Judith was gon from me and I was more lonesom—might help to forward one another in our Journey to Canaan.—Mr. Eyre[2] came within the door; I saluted him, ask'd how Mr. Clark did, and he went away. I took leave about 9 aclock. I told [her] I came now to refresh her Memory as to Monday night; said she had not forgot it. In discourse with her, I ask'd leave to speak with her Sister; I meant to gain Madam Mico's favour to persuade her Sister. She seem'd surpris'd and displeas'd, and said she was in the same condition! . . .

October 10. In the Evening I visited Madam Winthrop, who treated me with a great deal of

---

[2] A son of Madam Winthrop by her first marriage.

Curtesy; Wine, Marmalade. I gave her a News-Letter about the Thanksgiving; Proposals, for sake of the Verses for David Jeffries. She tells me Dr. Increase Mather visited her this day, in Mr. Hutchinson's Coach.

October 11. I writ a few Lines to Madam Winthrop to this purpose: "Madam, These wait on you with Mr. Mayhew's Sermon, and Account of the state of the Indians on Martha's Vinyard. I thank you for your Unmerited Favors of yesterday; and hope to have the Happiness of Waiting on you to-morrow before Eight a-clock after Noon. I pray GOD to keep you, and give you a joyfull entrance upon the Two Hundred and twenty-ninth year of Christopher Columbus his Discovery; and take Leave, who am, Madam, your humble Servant. S. S."

Sent this by Deacon Green, who deliver'd it to Sarah Chickering, her Mistress not being at home.

October 12. At Madam Winthrop's Steps I took leave of Capt Hill, &c. Mrs. Anne Cotton came to door (twas before 8.) said Madam Winthrop was within, directed me into the little Room, where she was full of work behind a Stand Mrs. Cotton came in and stood. Madam Winthrop pointed to her to set me a Chair. Madam Winthrop's Countenance was much changed from what 'twas on Monday, look'd dark and lowering. At last, the work, (black stuff or Silk) was taken away, I got my Chair in place, had some Converse, but very Cold and indifferent to what 'twas before. Ask'd her to acquit me of Rudeness if I drew off her Glove. Enquiring the reason, I told her twas great odds between handling a dead Goat, and a living Lady. Got it off. I told her I had one Petition to ask of her, that was, that she would take off the Negative she laid on me the third of October; She readily answer'd she could not, and enlarg'd upon it; She told me of it so soon as she could; could not leave her house, children, neighbours, business. I told her she might do som Good to help and support me. Mentioning Mrs. Gookin, Nath, the widow Weld was spoken of; said I had visited Mrs. Denison. I told her Yes! Afterward I said, If after a first and second Vagary she would Accept of me returning, Her Victorious Kindness and Good Will would be very Obliging. She thank'd me for my Book, (Mr. Mayhew's Sermon), But said not a word of the Letter. When she insisted on the Negative, I pray'd there might be no more Thunder and Lightening, I should not sleep all night. I gave her Dr. Preston, The Church's Marriage and the Church's Carriage, which cost me 6s. at the Sale. The door standing open, Mr. Airs came in, hung up His hat, and sat down. After awhile, Madam Winthrop moving, he went out. Jno. Eyre look'd in, I said How do ye, or your servant Mr. Eyre: but heard no word from him. Sarah fill'd a Glass of Wine, she drank to me, I to her, She sent Juno home with me with a good Lantern, I gave her 6d. and bid her thank her Mistress. In some of our Discourse, I told her I had rather go the Stone-House adjoining to her, than to come to her against her mind. Told her the reason why I came every other night was lest I should drink too deep draughts of Pleasure. She had talk'd of Canary, her Kisses were to me better than the

SAMUEL SEWALL

best Canary. Explain'd the expression Concerning Columbus.

October 13. I tell my Son and daughter Sewall, that the Weather was not so fair as I apprehended.

October 17. In the Evening I visited Madam Winthrop, who Treated me Courteously, but not in Clean Linen as somtimes. She said, she did not know whether I would come again, or no. I ask'd her how she could so impute inconstancy to me. (I had not visited her since Wednesday night being unable to get over the Indisposition received by the Treatment received that night, and *I must* in it seem'd to sound like a made piece of Formality.) Gave her this day's Gazett. Heard David Jeffries say the Lord's Prayer, and some other portions of the Scriptures. He came to the door, and ask'd me to go into Chamber, where his Grandmother was tending Little Katee, to whom she had given Physick; but I chose to sit below. Dr. Noyes and his wife came in, and sat a considerable time; had been visiting Son and daughter Cooper. Juno came home with me.

October 18. Visited Madam Mico, who came to me in a splendid Dress. I said, It may be you have heard of my Visiting Madam Winthrop, her Sister. She answered, Her Sister had told her of it. I ask'd her good Will in the Affair. She answer'd, If her Sister were for it, she should not hinder it. I gave her Mr. Homes's Sermon. She gave me a Glass of Canary, entertain'd me with good Discourse, and a Respectfull Remembrance of my first Wife. I took Leave.

October 19. Midweek, Visited Madam Winthrop; Sarah told me she was at Mr. Walley's, would not come home till late. I gave her Hannah 3 oranges with her Duty, not knowing whether I should find her or no. Was ready to go home: but said if I knew she was there, I would go thither. Sarah seem'd to speak with pretty good Courage, She would be there. I went and found her there, with Mr. Walley and his wife in the little Room below. At 7 a-clock I mentioned going home; at 8. I put on my Coat, and quickly waited on her home. She found occasion to speak loud to the servant, as if she had a mind to be known. Was Courteous to me; but took occasion to speak pretty earnestly about my keeping a Coach: I said 'twould cost £100. per annum: she said twould cost but £40. Spake much against John Winthrop, his false-heartedness. Mr. Eyre came in and sat awhile; I offer'd him Dr. Incr. Mather's Sermons, whereof Mr. Appleton's Ordination Sermon was one; said he had them already. I said I would give him another. Exit. Came away somewhat late.

October 20. Promis'd to wait on the Governor about 7. Madam Winthrop not being at Lecture, I went thither first; found her very Serene with her daughter Noyes, Mrs. Dering, and the widow Shipreev sitting at a little Table, she in her arm'd Chair. She drank to me, and I to Mrs. Noyes. After awhile pray'd the favor to speak with her. She took one of the Candles, and went into the best Room, clos'd the shutters, sat down upon the Couch. She told me Madam Usher had been there, and said the Coach must be set on Wheels, and not by Rusting. She spake something of my needing a Wigg. Ask'd me what her Sister said to me. I told her, She said, If her Sister were for it, She would not hinder it. But I told her, she did not say she would be glad to have me for her Brother. Said, I shall keep you in the Cold, and asked her if she would be within to morrow night, for we had had but a running Feat. She said she could not tell whether she should, or no. I took Leave. As were drinking at the Governour's, he said: In England the Ladies minded little more than that they might have Money, and Coaches to ride in. I said, And New-England brooks its Name. At which Mr. Dudley smiled. Governour said they were not quite so bad here.

October 21. Friday, My Son, the Minister, came to me P.M. by appointment and we pray one for another in the Old Chamber; more especially respecting my Courtship. About 6. a-clock I go to Madam Winthrop's; Sarah told me her Mistress was gon out, but did not tell me whither she went. She presently order'd me a Fire; so I went in, having Dr. Sibb's Bowels with me to read. I read the two first Sermons, still no body came in: at last about 9. a-clock Mr. Jno. Eyre came in; I took the opportunity to say to him as I had done to Mrs. Noyes before, that I hoped my Visiting his Mother would not be disagreeable to him; He answered me with much Respect. When twas after 9. a-clock He of himself said he would go and call her, she was but at one of his Brothers: A while after I heard Madam Winthrop's voice, enquiring somthing about John. After a good while and Clapping the Garden door twice or thrice, she came in. I mention'd somthing of the lateness; she banter'd me, and said I was later. She receiv'd me Courteously. I ask'd when our proceedings should be made publick: She said They were like to be no more publick than they were already. Offer'd me no Wine that I remember. I rose up at 11 a-clock to come away, saying I would put on my Coat, She offer'd not to help me. I pray'd her that Juno might light me home, she open'd the Shutter, and said 'twas pretty light abroad; Juno was weary and gon to bed. So I came home by Star-light as well as I could. At my first coming in, I gave Sarah five Shillings. I writ Mr. Eyre his name in his book with the date October 21, 1720. It cost me 8s. Jehovah jireh! Madam told me she had visited M. Mico, Wendell, and Wm. Clark of the South [Church].

October 22. Daughter Cooper visited me before my going out of Town, staid till about Sun set. I brought her going near as far as the Orange Tree. Coming back, near Leg's Corner, Little David Jeffries saw me, and looking upon me very lovingly, ask'd me if I was going to see his Grandmother? I said, Not to-night. Gave him a peny, and bid him present my Service to his Grandmother.

October 24. I went in the Hackny Coach through the Common, stop'd at Madam Winthrop's (had told her I would take my departure from thence). Sarah came to the door with Katee in her Arms: but I did not think to take notice of the Child. Call'd her Mistress. I told her, being encourag'd by David Jeffries loving eyes, and sweet Words, I was come to enquire whether she could find in her heart to leave that House and Neighbourhood, and go and dwell with me at the South-end; I think she said softly,

SAMUEL SEWALL

Not yet. I told her It did not ly in my Lands to keep a Coach. If I should, I should be in danger to be brought to keep company with her Neighbour Brooker, (he was a little before sent to prison for Debt). Told her I had an Antipathy against those who would pretend to give themselves; but nothing of their Estate. I would a proportion of my Estate with my self. And I supposed she would do so. As to a Perriwig, My best and greatest Friend, I could not possibly have a greater, began to find me with Hair before I was born, and had continued to do so ever since; and I could not find in my heart to go to another. She commended the book I gave her. Dr. Preston, the Church Marriage; quoted him saying 'twas inconvenient keeping out of a Fashion commonly used. I said the Time and Tide did circumscribe my Visit. She gave me a Dram of Black-Cherry Brandy, and gave me a lump of the Sugar that was in it. She wish'd me a good Journy. I pray'd God to keep her, and came away. Had a very pleasant Journy to Salem.

November 1. I was so taken up that I could not go if I would.

November 2. Midweek, went again, and found Mrs. Alden there, who quickly went out. Gave her about ½ pound of Sugar Almonds, cost 3s. per £. Carried them on Monday. She seem'd pleas'd with them, ask'd what they cost. Spake of giving her a Hundred pounds per annum if I dy'd before her. Ask'd her what sum she would give me, if she should dy first? Said I would give her time to Consider of it. She said she heard as if I had given all to my Children by Deeds of Gift. I told her 'twas a mistake, Point-Judith was mine &c. That in England I own'd, my Father's desire was that it should go to my eldest Son; 'twas 20£ per annum; she thought 'twas forty. I think when I seem'd to excuse pressing this, she seemed to think twas best to speak of it; a long winter was coming on. Gave me a Glass or two of Canary.

November 4. Friday, Went again, about 7. a-clock; found there Mr. John Walley and his wife: sat discoursing pleasantly. I shew'd them Isaac Moses's [an Indian] Writing. Madam W. serv'd Comfeits to us. After a-while a Table was spread, and Supper was set. I urg'd Mr. Walley to Crave a Blessing; but he put it upon me. About 9. they went away. I ask'd Madam what fashioned Neck-lace I should present her with, She said, None at all. I ask'd her Whereabout we left off last time; mention'd what I had offer'd to give her; Ask'd her what she would give me; She said she could not Change her Condition: She had said so from the beginning; could not be so far from her Children, the Lecture. Quoted the Apostle Paul affirming that a single Life was better than a Married. I answered That was for the present Distress. Said she had not pleasure in things of that nature as formerly: I said, you are the fitter to make me a Wife. If she held in that mind, I must go home and bewail my Rashness in making more haste than good Speed. However, considering the Supper, I desired her to be within next Monday night, if we liv'd so long. Assented. She charg'd me with saying, that she must put away Juno, if she came to me: I utterly deny'd it, it never came in my heart; yet she insisted upon it; saying it came in upon discourse about the Indian woman that obtained her Freedom this Court. About 10. I said I would not disturb the good orders of her House, and came away. She not seeming pleas'd with my Coming away. Spake to her about David Jeffries, had not seen him.

Monday, November 7. My Son pray'd in the Old Chamber. Our time had been taken up by Son and Daughter Cooper's Visit; so that I only read the 130th and 143. Psalm. Twas on the Account of my Courtship. I went to Mad. Winthrop; found her rocking her little Katee in the Cradle. I excus'd my Coming so late (near Eight). She set me an arm'd Chair and Cusheon; and so the Cradle was between her arm'd Chair and mine. Gave her the remnant of my Almonds; She did not eat of them as before; but laid them away; I said I came to enquire whether she had alter'd her mind since Friday, or remained of the same mind still. She said, Thereabouts. I told her I loved her, and was so fond as to think that she loved me: she said had a great respect for me. I told her, I had made her an offer, without asking any advice; she had so many to advise with, that 'twas an hindrance. The Fire was come to one short Brand besides the Block, which Brand was set up in end; at last it fell to pieces, and no Recruit was made: She gave me a glass of Wine. I think I repeated again that I would go home and bewail my Rashness in making more haste than good Speed. I would endeavor to contain myself, and not go on to sollicit her to do that which she could not

Consent to. Took leave of her. As came down the steps she bid me have a care. Treated me Courteously. Told her she had enter'd the 4th year of her Widowhood. I had given her the News-Letter before: I did not bid her draw off her Glove as sometime I had done. Her Dress was not so clean as somtime it had been. Jehovah Jireh.

Midweek, November 9th. Dine at Brother Stoddard's: were so kind as to enquire of me if they should invite Madam Winthrop; I answer'd No. Thank'd my Sister Stoddard for her Courtesie. Had a noble Treat. At night our Meeting was at the Widow Belknap's. Gave each one of the Meeting One of Mr. Holmes's Sermons, 12 in all; She sent her servant home with me with a Lantern. Madam Winthrop's Shutters were open as I pass'd by.

November 11th. Went not to Madam Winthrop's. This is the 2d Withdraw. . . .

About the middle of December Madam Winthrop made a Treat for her Children; Mr. Sewall, Prince, Willoughby: I knew nothing of it; but the same day abode in the Council Chamber for fear of the Rain, and din'd alone upon Kilby's Pyes and good Beer.[3]

[3] In the following summer Judge Sewall made his addresses to an old friend of his, then a widow, Mrs. Ruggles, by whom he was rejected. In March of the next year he married Mrs. Mary Gibbs.

COTTON MATHER

Born in Boston in 1663, died in 1728; son of Increase Mather; colleague of his father in the North Church of Boston in 1684, remaining in that pulpit until his death; active in the suppression of witchcraft; published his "Magnalia" in 1702, his "Wonders of the Invisible World" in 1692.

IN PRAISE OF JOHN ELIOT [1]

He that will write of Eliot must write of charity, or say nothing. His charity was a star of the first magnitude in the bright constellation of his vertues, and the rays of it were wonderfully various and extensive. His liberality to pious uses, whether publick or private, went much beyond the proportions of his little estate in the world. Many hundreds of pounds did he freely bestow upon the poor; and he would, with a very forcible importunity, press his neighbors to join with him in such beneficences. It was a marvelous alacrity with which he imbraced all opportunities of relieving any that were miserable; and the good people of Roxbury doubtless cannot remember (but the righteous God will!) how

[1] From the "Magnalia Christi Americana." This work comprises an ecclesiastical history of early New England, and has been in much favor with collectors. John Eliot has commonly been called "The Apostle of the Indians." He labored among them many years and translated into their language the Bible. Copies of the "Eliot Bible" are now among the most valuable of early American books.

often, and with what ardors, with what arguments, he became a beggar to them for collections in their assemblies, to support such needy objects as had fallen under his observation. The poor counted him their father, and repaired still unto him with a filial confidence in their necessities; and they were more than seven or eight, or indeed than so many scores, who received their portions of his bounty. Like that worthy and famous English general, he could not perswade himself "that he had anything but what he gave away," but he drove a mighty trade at such exercises as he thought would furnish him with bills of exchange, which he hoped "after many days" to find the comfort of; and yet, after all, he would say, like one of the most charitable souls that ever lived in the world, "that looking over his accounts he could nowhere find the God of heaven charged a debtor there." He did not put off his charity to be put in his last will, as many who therein shew that their charity is against their will; but he was his own administrator; he made his own hands his executors, and his own eyes his overseers. It has been remarked that liberal men are often long-lived men; so do they after many days find the bread with which they have been willing to keep other men alive. The great age of our Eliot was but agreeable to this remark; and when his age had unfitted him for almost all employments, and bereaved him of those gifts and parts which once he had been accomplished with, being asked, "How he did?" he would sometimes answer, "Alas, I have lost everything; my understanding leaves me, my memory fails me, my utterance fails me; but, I thank God, my charity holds out still; I find that rather grows than fails!" And I make no question, that at his death his happy soul was received and welcomed into the "everlasting habitations," by many scores got thither before him, of such as his charity had been liberal unto.

But besides these more substantial expressions of his charity, he made the odors of that grace yet more fragrant unto all that were about him, by that pitifulness and that peaceableness which rendered him yet further amiable. If any of his neighborhood were in distress, he was like a "brother born for their adversity," he would visit them, and comfort them with a most fraternal sympathy; yea, 'tis not easy to recount how many whole days of prayer and fasting he has got his neighbors to keep with him, on the behalf of those whose calamities he found himself touched withal. It was an extreme satisfaction to him that his wife had attained unto a considerable skill in physick and chirurgery, which enabled her to dispense many safe, good and useful medicines unto the poor that had occasion for them; and some hundreds of sick and weak and maimed people owed praises to God for the benefit which therein they freely received of her. The good gentleman her husband would still be casting oil into the flame of that charity, wherein she was of her own accord abundantly forward thus to be doing of good unto all; and he would urge her to be serviceable unto the worst enemies that he had in the world. Never had any man fewer enemies than he! but once having delivered something in his ministry which displeased one of his hearers, the man did passionately abuse him for it, and this both with speeches and with writings that reviled him. Yet it happening not long after that this man gave himself a very dangerous wound, Mr. Eliot immediately sends his wife to cure him; who did accordingly. When the man was well, he came to thank her, but she took no rewards; and this good man made him stay and eat with him, taking no notice of all the calumnies with which he had loaded him; but by this carriage he mollified and conquered the stomach of his reviler.

He was also a great enemy to all contention, and would ring aloud courfeu bell wherever he saw the fires of animosity. When he heard any ministers complain that such and such in their flocks were too difficult for them, the strain of his answer still was, "Brother, compass them!" and "Brother, learn the meaning of those three little words, bear, forbear, forgive." Yea, his inclinations for peace, indeed, sometimes almost made him to sacrifice right itself. When there was laid before an assembly of ministers a bundle of papers which contained certain matters of difference and contention between some people which our Eliot thought should rather unite, with an amnesty upon all their former quarrels, he (with some imitation of what Constantine did upon the like occasion) hastily threw the papers into the fire before them all, and, with a zeal for peace as hot as that fire, said immediately, "Brethren, wonder not at what I have done; I did it on my knees this morning before I came among you." Such an excess (if it were one) flowed from his charitable inclinations to be found among those peace-makers which, by following the example of that Man who is our peace, come to be called "the children of God." Very worthily might he be called an Irenæus as being all for peace; and the commendation which Epiphanius gives unto the ancient of that name, did belong unto our Eliot; he was "a most blessed and a most holy man." He disliked all sorts of bravery; but yet with an ingenious note upon the Greek word in Col. iii. 15, he propounded, "that peace might brave it among us." In short, wherever he came, it was like another old John, with solemn and earnest persuasives to love; and when he could say little else he would give that charge, "My children, love one another!"

Finally, 'twas his charity which disposed him to continual apprecations for, and benedictions on those that he met withal; he had an heart full of good wishes and a mouth full of kind blessings for them. And he often made his expressions very wittily agreeable to the circumstances which he saw the persons in. Sometimes when he came into a family, he would call for all the young people in it, that so he might very distinctly lay his holy hands upon every one of them, and bespeak the mercies of heaven for them all.

WILLIAM BYRD

Born in Virginia in 1674, died in 1744; educated in England and the Netherlands; visited the court of France; chosen a Fellow of the Royal Society; receiver-general of the revenue in Virginia and three times colonial agent for Virginia in England; for thirty-seven years member, and finally president, of the Council of Virginia; his home in Virginia the famous ancestral seat called Westover.

AT THE HOME OF COLONEL SPOTSWOOD[1]

SEPT., 1732. Colonel Spotswood's enchanted castle is on one side of the street, and a baker's dozen of ruinous tenements on the other, where so many German families had dwelt some years ago; but are now removed ten miles higher, in the Fork of Rappahannock, to land of their own. There had also been a chapel about a bow-shot from the colonel's house, at the end of an avenue of cherry trees, but some pious people had lately burned it down, with intent to get another built

[1] From "A Progress to the Mines," the date of the visit being 1732, which was the year in which Washington was born. Byrd's work is one of several admired writings by Byrd, now known collectively as the "Westover Manuscripts." Colonel Spotswood, of whom Byrd here writes, in early life had been a soldier under Marlborough, and in 1710 Governor of Virginia. In 1714, on his appointment to command a British expedition to the West Indies, he was made a major-general, but he died before embarking. He maintained fine establishments at Yorktown and on the Rapidan.

nearer to their own homes. Here I arrived about three o'clock, and found only Mrs. Spotswood at home, who received her old acquaintance with many a gracious smile. I was carried into a room elegantly set off with pier glasses, the largest of which came soon after to an odd misfortune. Amongst other favorite animals that cheered this lady's solitude, a brace of tame deer ran familiarly about the house, and one of them came to stare at me as a stranger. But unluckily spying his own figure in the glass, he made a spring over the tea-table that stood under it, and shattered the glass to pieces, and falling back upon the tea-table made a terrible fracas among the china.

This exploit was so sudden, and accompanied with such a noise, that it surprized me, and perfectly frightened Mrs. Spotswood. But 'twas worth all the damage to show the moderation and good humor with which she bore this disaster. In the evening the noble colonel came home from his mines, who saluted me very civilly, and Mrs. Spotswood's sister, Miss Theky, who had been to meet him *en cavalier*, was so kind too as to bid me welcome. We talked over a legend of old stories, supped about 9, and then prattled with the ladies, till it was time for a traveler to retire. In the mean time I observed my old friend to be very uxorious, and exceedingly fond of his children. This was so opposite to the maxims he used to preach up before he was married, that I could not forbear rubbing up the memory of them. But he gave a very good-natured turn to his change of sentiments by alleging that whoever brings a poor gentlewoman into so solitary a place, from all her friends and acquaintance, would be ungrateful not to use her and all that belongs to her with all possible tenderness.

We all kept snug in our several apartments till nine, except Miss Theky, who was the housewife of the family. At that hour we met over a pot of coffee, which was not quite strong enough to give us the palsy. After breakfast the colonel and I left the ladies to their domestic affairs, and took a turn in the garden, which has nothing beautiful but three terrace walks that fall in slopes one below another. I let him understand that, besides the pleasure of paying him a visit, I came to be instructed by so great a master in the mystery of making of iron, wherein he had led the way, and was the Tubal Cain of Virginia. He corrected me a little there, by assuring me he was not only the first in this country, but the first in North America who had erected a regular furnace. That they ran altogether upon bloomeries in New England and Pennsylvania till his example had made them attempt greater works. But in this last colony they have so few ships to carry their iron to Great Britain that they must be content to make it only for their own use, and must be obliged to manufacture it when they have done. That he hoped he had done the country very great service by setting so good an example. . . .

Our conversation on this subject continued till dinner, which was both elegant and plentiful. The afternoon was devoted to the ladies, who showed me one of their most beautiful walks. They conducted me through a shady lane to the landing, and by the way made me drink some very fine water that issued from a marble fountain, and ran incessantly. Just behind it was a covered bench, where Miss Theky often sat and bewailed her virginity. Then we proceeded to the river, which is the south branch of Rappahannock, about fifty yards wide, and so rapid that the ferry boat is drawn over by a chain, and therefore called the Rapidan. At night we drank prosperity to all the colonel's projects in a bowl of rack punch, and then retired to our devotions.

Having employed about two hours in retirement, I sallied out at the first summons to breakfast, where our conversation with the ladies, like whip syllabub, was very pretty, but had nothing in it. This, it seems, was Miss Theky's birthday, upon which I made her my compliments, and wished she might live twice as long a married woman as she had lived a maid. I did not presume to pry into the secret of her age, nor was she forward to disclose it, for this humble reason, lest I should think her wisdom fell short of her years. . . .

We had a Michaelmas goose for dinner, of Miss Theky's own raising, who was now good-natured enough to forget the jeopardy of her dog. In the afternoon we walked in a meadow by the river side, which winds in the form of a horseshoe about Germanna, making it a peninsula containing about four hundred acres. Rappahannock forks about fourteen miles below this place, the northern branch being the larger, and consequently must be the river that bounds my Lord Fairfax's grant of the northern neck.

The sun rose clear this morning, and so did I, and finished all my little affairs by breakfast. It was then resolved to wait on the ladies on horseback, since the bright sun, the fine air, and the wholesome exercise, all invited us to it. We forded the river a little above the ferry, and rode six miles up the neck to a fine level piece of rich land, where we found about twenty plants of ginseng, with the scarlet berries growing on the top of the middle stalk. The root of this is of wonderful virtue in many cases, particularly to raise the spirits and promote perspiration, which makes it a specific in colds and coughs. The colonel complimented me with all we found, in return for my telling him the virtues of it. We were all pleased to find so much of this king of plants so near the colonel's habitation, and growing, too, upon his own land; but were, however surprized to find it upon level ground, after we had been told it grew only upon the north side of Stony Mountains. I carried home this treasure with as much joy as if every root had been a graft of the Tree of Life, and washed and dried it carefully. This airing made us as hungry as so many hawks, so that between appetite and a very good dinner, 'twas difficult to eat like a philosopher. In the afternoon the ladies walked me about amongst all their little animals, with which they amuse themselves, and furnish the table; the worst of it is, they are so tenderhearted they shed a silent tear every time any of them are killed. At night the colonel and I quitted the threadbare subject of iron, and changed the scene to politics. He told me the ministry had receded from their demand upon

New England, to raise a standing salary for all succeeding governors, for fear some curious members of the House of Commons should inquire how the money was disposed of that had been raised in the other American colonies for the support of their governors. . . .

Our conversation was interrupted by a summons to supper, for the ladies, to show their power, had by this time brought us tamely to go to bed with our bellies full, tho we both at first declared positively against it. So very pliable a thing is frail man, when women have the bending of him.

JONATHAN EDWARDS

Born in Connecticut in 1703, died in Princeton in 1758; pastor at Northampton, Mass., in 1727-50; missionary to the Indians at Stockbridge in 1751-58; president of Princeton in 1758; his "Treatise Concerning the Religious Affections" published in 1746; "Qualifications for Full Communion" in 1749; "The Freedom of the Will," his most famous book, in 1754; "Doctrine of Original Sin Defended" in 1758, and "History of the Redemption" in 1772.

OF LIBERTY AND MORAL AGENCIES [1]

THE plain and obvious meaning of the words freedom and liberty, in common speech, is power, opportunity, or advantage, that any one has, to do as he pleases. Or, in other words, his being free from hindrance or impediment in the way of doing, or conducting in any respect, as he wills. (I say not only doing, but conducting; because a voluntary forbearing to do, sitting still, keeping silence, etc., are instances of persons' conduct, about which liberty is exercised; tho they are not so properly called

[1] From "The Freedom of the Will." It is not alone as a contribution to theology that this work has been much admired. It is probably the most famous theological treatise yet produced in America; one writer has called it "one of the most famous philosophical works in the world." But as an intellectual achievement solely, and for the perfection of its style, it has been quite as generally praised.

doing.) And the contrary to Liberty, whatever name we call that by, is a person's being hindered or unable to conduct as he will, or being necessitated to do otherwise.

If this which I have mentioned be the meaning of the word liberty, in the ordinary use of language; as I trust that none that has ever learned to talk, and is unprejudiced, will deny: then it will follow that in propriety of speech neither liberty, nor its contrary, can properly be ascribed to any being or thing but that which has such a faculty, power or property as is called will. For that which is possest of no such thing as will, can not have any power or opportunity of doing according to its will, nor be necessitated to act contrary to its will, nor be restrained from acting agreeably to it. And therefore to talk of liberty, or the contrary, as belonging to the very will itself is not to speak good sense; if we judge of sense and nonsense by the original and proper signification of words. For the will itself is not an agent that has a will: the power of choosing itself has not a power of choosing. That which has the power of volition or choice is the man or the soul, and not the power of volition itself. And he that has the liberty of doing according to his will, is the agent or doer who is possest of the will; and not the will which he is possest of. We say with propriety that a bird let loose has power and liberty to fly; but not that the bird's power of flying has a power and liberty of flying. To be free is the property of an agent, who is possest of powers and faculties, as much as to be cunning, valiant, bountiful, or zealous. But these qualities are the properties of men or persons and not the properties of properties.

There are two things that are contrary to this which is called liberty in common speech. One is constraint; the same is otherwise called force, compulsion, and coaction; which is a person's being necessitated to do a thing contrary to his will. The other is restraint; which is his being hindered, and not having power to do according to his will. But that which has no will, can not be the subject of these things. I need say the less on this head, Mr. Locke having set the same thing forth, with so great clearness, in his "Essay on the Human Understanding."

But one thing more I would observe concerning what is vulgarly called liberty; namely, that power and opportunity for one to do and conduct as he will, or according to his choice, is all that is meant by it; without taking into the meaning of the word anything of the cause or original of that choice; or at all considering how the person came to have such a volition; whether it was caused by some external motive or internal habitual bias; whether it was determined by some internal antecedent volition, or whether it happened without a cause; whether it was necessarily connected with something foregoing, or not connected. Let the person come by his volition or choice how he will, yet, if he is able, and there is nothing in the way to hinder his pursuing and executing his will, the man is fully and perfectly free, according to the primary and common notion of freedom.

What has been said may be sufficient to show what is meant by liberty, according to the com-

JONATHAN EDWARDS

mon notions of mankind, and in the usual and primary acceptation of the word: but the word, as used by Arminians, Pelagians and others, who oppose the Calvinists, has an entirely different signification. These several things belong to their notion of liberty. 1. That it consists in a self-determining power in the will, or a certain sovereignty the will has over itself, and its own acts, whereby it determines its own volitions; so as not to be dependent, in its determinations, on any cause without itself, nor determined by anything prior to its own acts. 2. Indifference belongs to liberty in their notion of it, or that the mind, previous to the act of volition, be in equilibrio. 3. Contingence is another thing that belongs and is essential to it; not in the common acceptation of the word, as that has been already explained, but as opposed to all necessity, or any fixt and certain connection with some previous ground or reason of its existence. They suppose the essence of liberty so much to consist in these things that unless the will of man be free in this sense, he has no real freedom, how much soever he may be at liberty to act according to his will.

A moral agent is a being that is capable of those actions that have a moral quality, and which can properly be denominated good or evil in a moral sense, virtuous or vicious, commendable or faulty. To moral agency belongs a moral faculty, or sense of moral good and evil, or of such a thing as desert or worthiness, of praise or blame, reward or punishment; and a capacity which an agent has of being influenced in his actions by moral inducements or motives, exhibited to the view of understanding and reason, to engage to a conduct agreeable to the moral faculty.

The sun is very excellent and beneficial in its action and influence on the earth, in warming it, and causing it to bring forth its fruits; but it is not a moral agent. Its action, tho good, is not virtuous or meritorious. Fire that breaks out in a city, and consumes great part of it, is very mischievous in its operation; but is not a moral agent. What it does is not faulty or sinful, or deserving of any punishment. The brute creatures are not moral agents. The actions of some of them are very profitable and pleasant; others are very hurtful; yet, seeing they have no moral faculty, or sense of desert, and do not act from choice guided by understanding, or with a capacity of reasoning and reflecting, but only from instinct, and are not capable of being influenced by moral inducements, their actions are not properly sinful or virtuous; nor are they properly the subjects of any such moral treatment for what they do, as moral agents are for their faults or good deeds.

Here it may be noted that there is a circumstantial difference between the moral agency of a ruler and a subject. I call it circumstantial, because it lies only in the difference of moral inducements they are capable of being influenced by, arising from the difference of circumstances. A ruler, acting in that capacity only, is not capable of being influenced by a moral law, and its sanctions of threatenings and promises, rewards and punishments as the subject is; tho both may be influenced by a knowledge of moral good and evil. And therefore the moral agency of the Supreme Being, who acts only in the capacity of a ruler toward His creatures, and never as a subject, differs in that respect from the moral agency of created intelligent beings. God's actions, and particularly those which are to be attributed to Him as moral governor, are morally good in the highest degree. They are most perfectly holy and righteous; and we must conceive of Him as influenced in the highest degree by that which, above all others, is properly a moral inducement, viz., the moral good which He sees in such and such things: and therefore He is, in the most proper sense, a moral agent, the source of all moral ability and agency, the fountain and rule of all virtue and moral good; tho by reason of His being supreme over all, it is not possible He should be under the influence of law or command, promises or threatenings, rewards or punishments, counsels or warnings. The essential qualities of a moral agent are in God, in the greatest possible perfection; such as understanding, to perceive the difference between moral good and evil; a capacity of discerning that moral worthiness and demerit, by which some things are praiseworthy, others deserving of blame and punishment; and also a capacity of choice, and choice guided by understanding, and a power of acting according to his choice or pleasure, and being capable of doing those things which are in the highest sense praiseworthy. And herein does very much consist that image of God wherein He made man (which we read of Gen. i. 26, 27, and chapter ix. 6), by which God distinguishes man from the beasts,

THE BEST OF THE WORLD'S CLASSICS

viz., in those faculties and principles of nature, whereby he is capable of moral agency. Herein very much consists the natural image of God; as His spiritual and moral image, wherein man was made at first, consisted in that moral excellency, that he was endowed with.

BENJAMIN FRANKLIN

Born in Boston in 1706, died in 1790; settled in Philadelphia in 1729; Postmaster of Philadelphia in 1737; discovered the identity of lightning with electricity in 1753; proposed a "Plan of Union" at Albany in 1754; Colonial Agent for Pennsylvania in England in 1757-62 and 1764-75; Member of the Second Continental Congress in 1775; Member of the Committee which drew up the Declaration of Independence in 1776; Ambassador to France in 1776; helped to negotiate the treaty of peace with England in 1783; President of Pennsylvania in 1785-88; Member of the Constitutional Convention in 1787.

I

HIS FIRST ENTRY INTO PHILADELPHIA[1]
(1729)

I HAVE been the more particular in this description of my journey, and shall be so of my first entry into that city, that you may in your mind compare such unlikely beginnings with the figure I have since made there. I was in my working dress, my best clothes being to come round by sea. I was dirty from my journey; my pockets were stuffed out with shirts and stockings, and I knew no soul nor where to look for lodging. I was fatigued with traveling, rowing and want of rest, I was very hungry; and my whole stock of cash consisted of a Dutch dollar, and about a shilling in copper. The latter I gave

[1] From Chapters I and II of the "Autobiography."

the people of the boat for my passage, who at first refused it, on account of my rowing; but I insisted on their taking it. A man being sometimes more generous when he has but a little money than when he has plenty, perhaps through fear of being thought to have but little.

Then I walked up the street, gazing about till near the market-house I met a boy with bread. I had made many a meal on bread, and, inquiring where he got it, I went immediately to the baker's he directed me to, in Second street, and asked for biscuit, intending such as we had in Boston; but they, it seems, were not made in Philadelphia. Then I asked for a three-penny loaf, and was told they had none such. So, not considering or knowing the difference of money, and the greater cheapness nor the names of his bread, I had him give me three pennyworth of any sort. He gave me, accordingly, three great puffy rolls. I was surprized at the quantity, but took it, and, having no room in my pockets, walked off with a roll under each arm, and eating the other. Thus I went up Market street as far as Fourth street, passing by the door of Mr. Read, my future wife's father;[2] when she, standing at the door, saw me, and thought I made, as I certainly did, a most awkward, ridiculous ap-

---

[2] Deborah was Mr. Read's daughter's name. Her grave, alongside Franklin's, in Philadelphia, has been a place of much pilgrimage these many years. One of the letters of Mrs. Franklin that has survived may be given here in illustration of her limited education. It was addrest to Franklin while he was in England, being dated "October ye 11, 1770":

"My dear Child:—the bairer of this is the Son of Dr. Phinis Bond his only son and a worthey young man he

BENJAMIN FRANKLIN

pearance. Then I turned and went down Chestnut street and part of Walnut street, eating my roll all the way, and, coming round, found myself again at Market street wharf, near the boat I came in, to which I went for a draft of the river water; and, being filled with one of my rolls, gave the other two to a woman and her child that came down the river in the boat with us, and were waiting to go farther.

Thus refreshed, I walked again up the street, which by this time had many clean-drest people in it, who were all walking the same way. I joined them, and thereby was led into the great meeting-house of the Quakers near the market. I sat down among them, and, after looking round awhile and hearing nothing said, being very drowsy through labor and want of rest the preceding night, I fell fast asleep, and continued so till the meeting broke up, when one was kind enough to rouse me. This was, therefore, the first house I was in, or slept in, in Philadelphia.

Walking down again toward the river, and, looking in the faces of people, I met a young Quaker man, whose countenance I liked, and, accosting him, requested he would tell me where a stranger could get lodging. We were then near the sign of the Three Mariners. "Here," says he, "is one place that entertains strangers, but

is going to studey the Law he desired a line to you I believe you have such a number of worthey young Jentelmen as ever wente to gather I hope to give you pleshner to see such a number of fine youthes from your one country which will be an Honour to thar parentes and Countrey.

"I am my dear Child your
    ffeckshonot
        Wife D. Franklin."

it is not a reputable house; if thee wilt walk with me, I'll show thee a better." He brought me to the Crooked Billet in Water street. Here I got a dinner; and, while I was eating it, several sly questions were asked me, as it seemed to be suspected, from my youth and appearance, that I might be some runaway.

After dinner, my host having shown me to a bed, I laid myself on without undressing, and slept till six in the evening, when I was called to supper. I went to bed again very early, and slept very soundly till next morning. Then I drest myself as neat as I could, and went to Andrew Bradford the printer's. I found in the shop the old man his father, whom I had seen at New York, and who, traveling on horseback, had got to Philadelphia before me. He introduced me to his son, who received me civilly, gave me a breakfast, but told me he did not at present want a hand, being lately supplied with one; but there was another printer in town, lately set up, one Keimer, who, perhaps, might employ me; if not, I should be welcome to lodge at his house, and he would give me a little work to do now and then till fuller business should offer.

II

WARNINGS BRADDOCK DID NOT HEED [3]

This general [Braddock] was, I think, a brave man, and might probably have made a figure as a good officer in some European war. But he had too much self-confidence, too high an opinion of the validity of regular troops, and too mean a one of both Americans and Indians. George Croghan,[4] our Indian interpreter, joined him on his march with one hundred of those people, who might have been of great use to his army as guides, scouts, etc., if he had treated them kindly; but he slighted and neglected them, and they gradually left him.

In conversation with him one day he was giving me some account of his intended progress. "After taking Fort Duquesne,"[5] says he, "I am to proceed to Niagara; and, having taken that, to

[3] From Chapter X of the "Autobiography."

[4] Croghan afterward became associated closely with Sir William Johnson in the Mohawk and Upper Susquehanna Valleys. He acquired title to a large tract of land at the foot of Otsego Lake, but, while settling it, mortgaged the land heavily, and eventually lost it through foreclosure. William Cooper, father of the novelist, subsequently obtained title to these lands and went into the country to settle them. In the course of his labors, he founded the village of Cooperstown, and made it his home. It was this circumstance which led to Fenimore Cooper's knowledge of Indian and frontier life as depicted in his writings. The home of William Cooper had previously been in Burlington, N. J.

[5] Now Pittsburg.

Frontenac,[6] if the season will allow time; and I suppose it will, for Duquesne can hardly detain me above three or four days; and then I see nothing that can obstruct my march to Niagara." Having before revolved in my mind the long line his army must make in their march by a very narrow road, to be cut for them through the woods and bushes, and also what I had read of a former defeat of fifteen hundred French, who invaded the Iroquois country, I had conceived some doubts and some fears for the event of the campaign. But I ventured only to say, "To be sure, sir, if you arrive well before Duquesne, with these fine troops, so well provided with artillery, that place, not yet completely fortified and as we hear with no very strong garrison, can probably make but a short resistance. The only danger I apprehend of obstruction to your march is from ambuscades of Indians, who, by constant practise, are dextrous in laying and executing them; and the slender line, near four miles long, which your army must make, may expose it to be attacked by surprize in its flanks, and to be cut like a thread into several pieces, which, from their distance, can not come up in time to support each other."

He smiled at my ignorance, and replied, "These savages may, indeed, be a formidable enemy to your raw American militia, but upon the King's regular and disciplined troops, sir, it is impossible they should make any impression." I was

[6] In early times commonly called Fort Frontenac, but now Kingston, Ontario, Canada. The name was changed to Kingston by Loyalists who settled at the fort after the American Revolution.

BENJAMIN FRANKLIN

conscious of an impropriety in my disputing with a military man in matters of his profession, and said no more. The enemy, however, did not take advantage of his army which I apprehended its long line of march exposed it to, but let it advance without interruption till within nine miles of the place; and then, when more in a body (for it had just passed a river, where the front had halted till all were come over), and in a more open part of the woods than any it had passed, attacked its advanced guard by a heavy fire from behind trees and bushes, which was the first intelligence the general had of an enemy's being near him. This guard being disordered, the general hurried the troops up to their assistance, which was done in great confusion, through wagons, baggage, and cattle; and presently the fire came upon their flank: the officers, being on horseback, were more easily distinguished, picked out as marks, and fell very fast; and the soldiers were crowded together in a huddle, having or hearing no orders, and standing to be shot at till two-thirds of them were killed; and then, being seized with a panic, the whole fled with precipitation.

The wagoners took each a horse out of his team and scampered; their example was immediately followed by others; so that all the wagons, provisions, artillery, and stores were left to the enemy. The general, being wounded, was brought off with difficulty; his secretary, Mr. Shirley, was killed by his side; and out of eighty-six officers, sixty-three were killed or wounded, and seven hundred and fourteen men killed out of eleven hundred. These eleven hundred had been picked men from the whole army; the rest had been left behind with Colonel Dunbar, who was to follow with the heavier part of the stores, provisions, and baggage. The flyers, not being pursued, arrived at Dunbar's camp, and the panic they brought with them instantly seized him and all his people; and, tho he had now above one thousand men, and the enemy who had beaten Braddock did not at most exceed four hundred Indians and French together, instead of proceeding, and endeavoring to recover some of the lost honor, he ordered all the stores, ammunition, etc., to be destroyed, that he might have more horses to assist his flight toward the settlements, and less lumber to remove. He was there met with requests from the governors of Virginia, Maryland and Pennsylvania that he would post his troops on the frontiers, so as to afford some protection to the inhabitants; but he continued his hasty march through all the country, not thinking himself safe till he arrived at Philadelphia, where the inhabitants could protect him. This whole transaction gave us Americans the first suspicion that our exalted ideas of the prowess of British regulars had not been well founded.

In their first march, too, from their landing till they got beyond the settlements, they had plundered and stript the inhabitants, totally ruining some poor families, besides insulting, abusing, and confining the people if they remonstrated. This was enough to put us out of conceit of such defenders, if we had really wanted any. How different was the conduct of our French friends in 1781, who, during a march through the most inhabited part of our country, from Rhode Island to Virginia, near seven hundred miles, occasioned not the smallest complaint for the loss of a pig, a chicken, or even an apple.

III

HOW TO DRAW LIGHTNING FROM THE CLOUDS[7]

As frequent mention is made in public papers from Europe of the success of the Philadelphia experiment for drawing the electric fire from clouds by means of pointed rods of iron erected on high buildings, etc., it may be agreeable to the curious to be informed that the same experiment has succeeded in Philadelphia, tho made in a different and more easy manner, which is as follows.

Make a small cross of two light strips of cedar, the arms so long as to reach to the four corners of a large thin silk handkerchief when extended; tie the corners of the handkerchief to the extremities of the cross, so you have the body of a kite; which, being properly accommodated with a tail, loop, and string, will rise in the air, like those made of paper; but this being of silk is fitter to bear the wet and wind of a thunder-gust without tearing. To the top of the upright stick of the cross is to be fixt a very sharp-pointed wire, rising a foot or more above the wood. To

[7] From a letter to Peter Collinson, dated October 19, 1752, and read before the Royal Society of London in December of the same year.

the end of the twine, next the hand, is to be tied a silk ribbon, and where the silk and twine join, a key may be fastened. This kite is to be raised when a thunder-gust appears to be coming on, and the person who holds the string must stand within a door or window, or under some cover, so that the silk ribbon may not be wet; and care must be taken that the twine does not touch the frame of the door or window. As soon as any of the thunder-clouds come over the kite, the pointed wire will draw the electric fire from them, and the kite, with all the twine, will be electrified, and the loose filaments of the twine will stand out every way, and be attracted by an approaching finger. And when the rain has wetted the kite and twine, so that it can conduct the electric fire freely, you will find it stream out plentifully from the key on the approach of your knuckle. At this key the vial may be charged; and from electric fire thus obtained, spirits may be kindled, and all the other electric experiments be performed, which are usually done by the help of a rubbed glass globe or tube, and thereby the sameness of the electric matter with that of lightning completely demonstrated.

BENJAMIN FRANKLIN

IV

THE WAY TO WEALTH[8]

COURTEOUS reader:

I have heard that nothing gives an author so great pleasure as to find his works respectfully quoted by others. Judge, then, how much I must have been gratified by an incident I am going to relate to you. I stopt my horse lately, where a great number of people were collected at an auction of merchants' goods. The hour of the sale not being come, they were conversing on the badness of the times; and one of the company called to a plain, clean old man, with white locks, "Pray, Father Abraham, what think you of the times? Will not these heavy taxes quite ruin the country? How shall we ever be able to pay them? What would you advise us to do?" Father Abraham stood up and replied, "If you would have my advice, I will give it you in short; for 'A word to the wise is enough,' as Poor Richard says." They joined in desiring him to speak his mind, and gathering round him he proceeded as follows.

"Friends," said he, "the taxes are indeed very

[8] From "Poor Richard's Almanac" for 1757, where it was printed as a preface signed "Richard Saunders." Franklin began this Almanac in 1732. John Bigelow, Franklin's biographer and editor, says it "attained an astonishing popularity." For twenty-five years it had an average circulation of 10,000 copies. Sometimes it was sent to press as early as October in order to supply remote colonists in time for the new year. Translations of it have been printed in nearly all written languages.

heavy, and, if those laid on by the government were the only ones we had to pay, we might more easily discharge them; but we have many others, and much more grievous to some of us. We are taxed twice as much by our idleness, three times as much by our pride, and four times as much by our folly; and from these taxes the commissioners can not ease or deliver us by allowing an abatement. However, let us harken to good advice, and something may be done for us; 'God helps them that help themselves,' as Poor Richard says.

"I. It would be thought a hard government that should tax its people one-tenth part of their time, to be employed in its service; but idleness taxes many of us much more; sloth, by bringing on diseases, absolutely shortens life. 'Sloth, like rust, consumes faster than labor wears; while the used key is always bright,' as Poor Richard says. 'But dost thou love life, then do not squander time, for that is the stuff life is made of,' as Poor Richard says. How much more than is necessary do we spend in sleep, forgetting that 'The sleeping fox catches no poultry,' and that 'There will be sleeping enough in the grave,' as Poor Richard says.

" 'If time be of all things the most precious, wasting time must be,' as Poor Richard says, 'the greatest prodigality'; since, as he elsewhere tells us, 'Lost time is never found again; and what we call time enough, always proves little enough.' Let us, then, up and be doing, and doing to the purpose; so by diligence shall we do more with less perplexity. 'Sloth makes all things difficult, but industry all easy'; and 'He that riseth late

BENJAMIN FRANKLIN

must trot all day, and shall scarce overtake his business at night'; while 'Laziness travels so slowly that Poverty soon overtakes him. Drive thy business, let not that drive thee'; and 'Early to bed, and early to rise, makes a man healthy, wealthy, and wise,' as Poor Richard says. . . .

"Methinks I hear some of you say, 'Must a man afford himself no leisure?' I will tell thee, my friend, what Poor Richard says, 'Employ thy time well, if thou meanest to gain leisure; and, since thou art not sure of a minute, throw not away an hour.' Leisure is time for doing something useful; this leisure the diligent man will obtain, but the lazy man never; for 'A life of leisure and a life of laziness are two things. Many, without labor, would live by their wits only, but they break for want of stock'; whereas industry gives comfort, and plenty, and respect. 'Fly pleasures, and they will follow you. The diligent spinner has a large shift; and now I have a sheep and a cow, everybody bids me good morrow.'

"II. But with our industry we must likewise be steady, settled, and careful, and oversee our own affairs with our own eye, and not trust too much to others; for, as Poor Richard says,

'I never saw an oft-removed tree,
  Nor yet an oft-removed family,
  That throve so well as those that settled be.'

And again, 'Three removes are as bad as a fire'; and again, 'Keep thy shop, and thy shop will keep thee'; and again, 'If you would have your business done, go; if not, send.' And again,

'He that by the plough would thrive,
  Himself must either hold or drive.'

And again, 'The eye of a master will do more work than both his hands'; and again, 'Want of care does us more damage than want of knowledge'; and again, 'Not to oversee workmen, is to leave them your purse open.' Trusting too much to others' care is the ruin of many; for 'In the affairs of this world men are saved not by faith, but by the want of it'; but a man's own care is profitable; for 'If you would have a faithful servant, and one that you like, serve yourself. A little neglect may breed great mischief; for want of a nail the shoe was lost; for want of a shoe the horse was lost; and for want of a horse the rider was lost, being overtaken and slain by the enemy; all for want of a little care about a horseshoe nail.'

"III. So much for industry, my friends, and attention to one's own business; but to these we must add frugality, if we would make our industry more certainly successful. A man may, if he knows not how to save as he gets, keep his nose all his life to the grindstone, and die not worth a groat at last. 'A fat kitchen makes a lean will'; and

'Many estates are spent in the getting,
  Since women for tea forsook spinning and knitting,
  And men for punch forsook hewing and splitting.'

'If you would be wealthy, think of saving as well as of getting. The Indies have not made Spain rich, because her outgoes are greater than her incomes.'

"Away, then, with your expensive follies, and you will not then have so much cause to complain of hard times, heavy taxes, and chargeable families; for

'Women and wine, game and deceit,
Make the wealth small and the want great.'

"And further, 'What maintains one vice would bring up two children.' You may think, perhaps, that a little tea, or a little punch now and then, diet a little more costly, clothes a little finer, and a little entertainment now and then can be no great matter; but remember, 'Many a little makes a mickle.' Beware of little expenses; 'A small leak will sink a great ship,' as Poor Richard says; and again, 'Who dainties love, shall beggars prove'; and moreover, 'Fools makes feasts, and wise men eat them. . . . If you would know the value of money, go and try to borrow some; for he that goes a-borrowing goes a-sorrowing,' as Poor Richard says; and, indeed, so does he that lends to such people, when he goes to get it in again. Poor Dick further advises, and says,

'Fond pride of dress is sure a very curse;
Ere fancy you consult, consult your purse.'

And again, 'Pride is as loud a beggar as Want, and a great deal more saucy.' When you have bought one fine thing, you must buy ten more, that your appearance may be all of a piece; but Poor Dick says, 'It is easier to suppress the first desire than to satisfy all that follow it.' And it is as truly folly for the poor to ape the rich as for the frog to swell in order to equal the ox.

'Vessels large may venture more,
But little boats should keep near shore.'

It is, however, a folly soon punished; for, as Poor Richard says, 'Pride that dines on vanity sups on contempt. Pride breakfasted with Plenty, dined with Poverty, and supped with Infamy.' And, after all, of what use is this pride of appearance, for which so much is risked, so much is suffered? It can not promote health, nor ease pain; it makes no increase of merit in the person; it creates envy; it hastens misfortune.

"But what madness must it be to run in debt for these superfluities. . . . When you have got your bargain, you may, perhaps, think little of payment; but, as Poor Richard says, 'Creditors have better memories than debtors; creditors are a superstitious sect, great observers of set days and times.' The day comes round before you are aware, and the demand is made before you are prepared to satisfy it; or, if you bear your debt in mind, the term, which at first seemed so long, will, as it lessens, appear extremely short. Time will seem to have added wings to his heels as well as his shoulders. 'Those have a short Lent who owe money to be paid at Easter.' At present, perhaps, you may think yourselves in thriving circumstances, and that you can bear a little extravagance without injury; but

'For age and want save while you may;
No morning sun lasts a whole day.'

Gain may be temporary and uncertain, but ever, while you live, expense is constant and certain; and 'It is easier to build two chimneys than to keep one in fuel,' as Poor Richard says; so, 'Rather go to bed supperless than rise in debt.'

'Get what you can, and what you get hold;
   'Tis the stone that will turn all your lead into gold.'

And when you have got the philosopher's stone, sure you will no longer complain of bad times, or the difficulty of paying taxes.

"IV. This doctrine, my friends, is reason and wisdom; but, after all, do not depend too much upon your own industry, and frugality, and prudence, tho excellent things; for they may all be blasted without the blessing of Heaven; and, therefore, ask that blessing humbly, and be not uncharitable to those that at present seem to want it, but comfort and help them. Remember, Job suffered, and was afterward prosperous.

"And now, to conclude, 'Experience keeps a dear school, but fools will learn in no other,' as Poor Richard says, and scarce in that; for, it is true, 'We may give advice, but we can not give conduct.' However, remember this, 'They that will not be counseled, can not be helped;' and further, that 'If you will not hear Reason, she will surely rap your knuckles' as Poor Richard says."

Thus the old gentleman ended his harangue. The people heard it and approved the doctrine; and immediately practised the contrary, just as if it had been a common sermon; for the auction opened, and they began to buy extravagantly.

I found the good man had thoroughly studied my Almanacs, and digested all I had dropt on these topics during the course of twenty-five years. The frequent mention he made of me must have tired any one else; but my vanity was wonderfully delighted with it, tho I was conscious that not a tenth part of the wisdom was my own, which he ascribed to me, but rather the gleanings that I had made of the sense of all ages and nations. However, I resolved to be the better for the echo of it; and tho I had at first determined to buy stuff for a new coat, I went away resolved to wear my old one a little longer. Reader, if thou wilt do the same, thy profit will be as great as mine.

V

A DIALOG WITH THE GOUT
[*Dated at midnight, 22 October, 1780.*]

FRANKLIN. Eh! Oh! Eh! What have I done to merit these cruel sufferings?

Gout. Many things; you have ate and drank too freely, and too much indulged those legs of yours in their indolence.

Franklin. Who is it that accuses me?

Gout. It is I, even I, the Gout.

Franklin. What! my enemy in person?

Gout. No, not your enemy.

Franklin. I repeat it; my enemy; for you would not only torment my body to death, but ruin my good name; you reproach me as a glutton and

BENJAMIN FRANKLIN

a tippler; now all the world that knows me will allow that I am neither the one nor the other.

Gout. The world may think as it pleases; it is always very complaisant to itself, and sometimes to its friends; but I very well know that the quantity of meat and drink proper for a man who takes a reasonable degree of exercise, would be too much for another, who never takes any.

Franklin. I take—Eh! Oh!—as much exercise —Eh!—as I can, Madam Gout. You know my sedentary state, and on that account, it would seem, Madam Gout, as if you might spare me a little, seeing it is not altogether my own fault.

Gout. Not a jot; your rhetoric and your politeness are thrown away; your apology avails nothing. If your situation in life is a sedentary one, your amusements, your recreations, at least, should be active. You ought to walk or ride; or, if the weather prevents that, play at billiards. But let us examine your course of life. While the mornings are long, and you have leisure to go abroad, what do you do? Why, instead of gaining an appetite for breakfast, by salutary exercise, you amuse yourself with books, pamphlets, or newspapers, which commonly are not worth the reading. Yet you eat an inordinate breakfast, four dishes of tea, with cream, and one or two buttered toasts, with slices of hung beef, which I fancy are not things the most easily digested. Immediately afterward you sit down to write at your desk, or converse with persons who apply to you on business. Thus the time passes till one, without any kind of bodily exercise.

But all this I could pardon, in regard, as

you say, to your sedentary condition. But what is your practise after dinner? Walking in the beautiful gardens of those friends with whom you have dined would be the choice of men of sense; yours is to be fixt down to chess, where you are found engaged for two or three hours! This is your perpetual recreation, which is the least eligible of any for a sedentary man, because, instead of accelerating the motion of the fluids, the rigid attention it requires helps to retard the circulation and obstruct internal secretions. Wrapt in the speculations of this wretched game, you destroy your constitution. What can be expected from such a course of living but a body replete with stagnant humors, ready to fall a prey to all kinds of dangerous maladies, if I, the Gout, did not occasionally bring you relief by agitating those humors, and so purifying or dissipating them? If it was in some nook or alley in Paris, deprived of walks, that you played awhile at chess after dinner, this might be excusable; but the same taste prevails with you in Passy, Auteuil, Montmartre, or Sanoy, places where there are the finest gardens and walks, a pure air, beautiful women, and most agreeable and instructive conversation; all which you might enjoy by frequenting the walks. But these are rejected for this abominable game of chess. Fie, then, Mr. Franklin! But amidst my instructions, I had almost forgot to administer my wholesome corrections; so take that twinge—and that.

Franklin. Oh! Eh! Oh! Ohhh! As much instruction as you please, Madam Gout, and as many reproaches; but pray, Madam, a truce with your corrections!

BENJAMIN FRANKLIN

Gout. No, Sir, no—I will not abate a particle of what is so much for your good—therefore—

Franklin. Oh! Ehhh!—It is not fair to say I take no exercise, when I do very often, going out to dine and returning in my carriage.

Gout. That, of all imaginable exercises, is the most slight and insignificant, if you allude to the motion of a carriage suspended on springs. By observing the degree of heat obtained by different kinds of motion we may form an estimate of the quantity of exercise given by each. Thus, for example, if you turn out to walk in winter with cold feet, in an hour's time you will be in a glow all over; ride on horseback, the same effect will scarcely be perceived by four hours' round trotting; but if you loll in a carriage, such as you have mentioned, you may travel all day, and gladly enter the last inn to warm your feet by a fire. Flatter yourself then no longer that half an hour's airing in your carriage deserves the name of exercise. Providence has appointed few to roll in carriages, while he has given to all a pair of legs, which are machines infinitely more commodious and serviceable. Be grateful, then, and make a proper use of yours. Would you know how they forward the circulation of your fluids, in the very action of transporting you from place to place; observe when you walk that all your weight is alternately thrown from one leg to the other; this occasions a great pressure on the vessels of the foot, and repels their contents; when relieved, by the weight being thrown on the other foot, the vessels of the first are allowed to replenish, and, by a return of this weight, this repulsion again succeeds, thus accelerating the circulation of the blood. The heat produced in any given time depends on the degree of this acceleration; the fluids are shaken, the humors attenuated, the secretions facilitated, and all goes well; the cheeks are ruddy, and health is established. Behold your fair friend at Auteuil;[9] a lady who received from bounteous nature more really useful science than half a dozen of such pretenders to philosophy as you have been able to extract from all your books. When she honors you with a visit, it is on foot. She walks all hours of the day, and leaves indolence, and its concomitant maladies, to be endured by her horses. In this see at once the preservative of her health and personal charms. But when you go to Auteuil, you must have your carriage, tho it is no farther from Passy to Auteuil than from Auteuil to Passy.

Franklin. Your reasonings grow very tiresome.

Gout. I stand corrected. I will be silent and continue my office; take that, and that.

Franklin. Oh! Ohh! Talk on, I pray you.

Gout. No, no; I have a good number of twinges for you to-night, and you may be sure of some more to-morrow.

Franklin. What, with such a fever! I shall go distracted. Oh! Eh! Can no one bear it for me?

---

[9] The reference is to Madame Helvetius, whom Franklin knew as the widow of the writer Claude Adrien Helvetius. Her home was long a center of literary society in France. The friendship with Franklin was a notable incident in his career as American Ambassador to France. See his letter to her printed here as the sixth of these selections from Franklin.

Gout. Ask that of your horses; they have served you faithfully.

Franklin. How can you so cruelly sport with my torments?

Gout. Sport! I am very serious. I have here a list of offenses against your own health distinctly written, and can justify every stroke inflicted on you.

Franklin. Read it then.

Gout. It is too long a detail; but I will briefly mention some particulars.

Franklin. Proceed. I am all attention.

Gout. Do you remember how often you have promised yourself, the following morning, a walk in the grove of Boulogne, in the garden de la Muette, or in your own garden, and have violated your promise, alleging at one time it was too cold, at another too warm, too windy, too moist, or what else you pleased; when in truth it was too nothing but your insuperable love of ease?

Franklin. That I confess may have happened occasionally, probably ten times in a year.

Gout. Your confession is very far short of the truth; the gross amount is one hundred and ninety-nine times.

Franklin. Is it possible?

Gout. So possible that it is fact; you may rely on the accuracy of my statement. You know Mr. Brillon's gardens, and what fine walks they contain; you know the handsome flight of a hundred steps, which lead from the terrace above to the lawn below. You have been in the practise of visiting this amiable family twice a week, after dinner, and it is a maxim of your own, that "a man may take as much exercise in walking a mile up- and down-stairs as in ten on level ground." What an opportunity was here for you to have had exercise in both these ways! Did you embrace it, and how often?

Franklin. I can not immediately answer that question.

Gout. I will do it for you; not once.

Franklin. Not once?

Gout. Even so. During the summer you went there at six o'clock. You found the charming lady, with her lovely children and friends, eager to walk with you, and entertain you with their agreeable conversation; and what has been your choice? Why, to sit on the terrace, satisfying yourself with the fine prospect, and passing your eye over the beauties of the garden below, without taking one step to descend and walk about in them.

On the contrary, dear sir, you call for tea and the chess-board; and lo! you are occupied in your seat till nine o'clock, and that besides two hours' play after dinner; and then, instead of walking home, which would have bestirred you a little, you step into your carriage. How absurd to suppose that all this carelessness can be reconcilable with health, without my interposition!

Franklin. I am convinced now of the justness of Poor Richard's remark that "Our debts and our sins are always greater than we think for."

Gout. So it is. You philosophers are sages in your maxims, and fools in your conduct.

Franklin. But do you charge, among my crimes, that I return in a carriage from Mr. Brillon's?

Gout. Certainly; for having been seated all the while, you can not object the fatigue of the day, and can not want, therefore, the relief of a carriage.

Franklin. What, then, would you have me do with my carriage?

Gout. Burn it, if you choose; you would at least get heat out of it once in this way, or, if you dislike that proposal, here's another for you; observe the poor peasants, who work in the vineyards and grounds about the villages of Passy, Auteuil, Chaillot, etc.; you may find every day, among these deserving creatures, four or five old men and women, bent and perhaps crippled by weight of years and too long and too great labor. After a most fatiguing day, these people have to trudge a mile or two to their smoky huts. Order your coachman to set them down. This is an act that will be good for your soul; and, at the same time, after your visit to the Brillons, if you return on foot, that will be good for your body.

Franklin. Ah! how tiresome you are!

Gout. Well, then, to my office; it should not be forgotten that I am your physician. There.

Franklin. Ohhh! what a devil of a physician!

Gout. How ungrateful you are to say so! Is it not I who, in the character of your physician, have saved you from the palsy, dropsy and apoplexy? one or other of which would have done for you long ago but for me.

Franklin. I submit, and thank you for the past, but entreat the discontinuance of your visits for the future; for, in my mind, one had better die than be cured so dolefully. Permit me just to hint that I have also not been unfriendly to you. I never feed physician or quack of any kind, to enter the list against you; if, then, you do not leave me to my repose, it may be said you are ungrateful too.

Gout. I can scarcely acknowledge that as any objection. As to quacks, I despise them; they may kill you, indeed, but can not injure me. And as to regular physicians, they are at last convinced that the gout, in such a subject as you are, is no disease, but a remedy; and wherefore cure a remedy?—but to our business—there.

Franklin. Oh! Oh!—for Heaven's sake leave me; and I promise faithfully never more to play at chess, but to take exercise daily, and live temperately.

Gout. I know you too well. You promise fair; after a few months of good health you will return to your old habits; your fine promises will be forgotten like the forms of the last year's clouds. Let us then finish the account, and I will go. But leave you with an assurance of visiting you again at a proper time and place; for my object is your good, and you are sensible now that I am your real friend.

VI

A PROPOSAL TO MADAME HELVETIUS [10]

Mortified at the barbarous resolution pronounced by you so positively yesterday evening, that you would remain single for the rest of your life as a compliment due to the memory of your

[10] A letter now printed in Volume VI of the "Works of Franklin," edited by John Bigelow.

husband, I retired to my chamber. Throwing myself upon my bed I dreamt that I was dead, and was transported to the Elysian fields.

I was asked whether I wished to see any persons in particular; to which I replied that I wished to see the philosophers. "There are two who live here at hand in this garden; they are good neighbors and very friendly toward one another." "Who are they?" "Socrates and Helvetius." "I esteem them both highly; but let me see Helvetius first, because I understand a little French but not a word of Greek." I was conducted to him; he received me with much courtesy, having known me, he said, by character some time past. He asked me a thousand questions relative to the war, the present state of religion, of liberty, of the government in France. "You do not inquire, then," said I, "after your dear friend, Madame Helvetius; yet she loves you exceedingly. I was in her company not more than an hour ago." "Ah," said he, "you make me recur to my past happiness, which ought to be forgotten in order to be happy here. For many years I could think of nothing but her, tho at length I am consoled. I have taken another wife, the most like her that I could find; she is not, indeed, altogether so handsome, but she has a great fund of wit and good sense, and her whole study is to please me. She is at this moment gone to fetch the nectar and ambrosia to regale me; stay here awhile and you will see her." "I perceive," said I, "that your former friend is more faithful to you than you are to her; she has had several good offers, but has refused them all. I will confess to you that I love her extremely, but she was cruel to me and rejected me peremptorily for your sake." "I pity you sincerely," said he, "for she is an excellent woman, handsome and amiable. But do not the Abbe de la R— and the Abbe M— visit her?" "Certainly they do; not one of your friends has dropt her acquaintance." "If you had gained the Abbe M— with a bribe of good coffee and cream perhaps you would have succeeded; for he is as deep a reasoner as Dun Scotus or St. Thomas; he arranges and methodizes his arguments in such a manner that they are almost irresistible. Or if by a fine edition of some old classic you had gained the Abbe de la R— to speak against you, that would have been still better, as I always observed that when he recommended anything to her, she had a great inclination to do exactly the contrary."

As he finished these words the new Madame Helvetius entered with the nectar and I recognized her immediately as my former American friend, Mrs. Franklin! I reclaimed her, but she answered me coldly, "I was a good wife to you for forty-nine years and four months, nearly half a century; let that content you. I have formed a new condition here, which will last to eternity."

Indignant at this refusal of my Eurydice, I immediately resolved to quit those ungraceful shades and return to this good world again, to behold the sun and you. Here am I, let us *avenge ourselves.*

GEORGE WASHINGTON

Born in 1732, died in 1799; adjutant of Virginia troops in 1751; sent on a mission to the French beyond the Alleghany River in 1753; defended Fort Necessity in 1754; with Braddock at his defeat in 1755; led the advance guard to Fort Duquesne in 1758; Member of the Continental Congress in 1774-75; made Commander-in-chief of the Continental Army in 1775; resigned his commission in 1783; President of the Constitutional Convention in 1787; elected President of the United States in 1789; reelected President in 1793; Commander-in-chief of the Army in 1798.

I

TO HIS WIFE ON TAKING COMMAND OF THE ARMY[1]

MY DEAREST: I am now set down to write to you on a subject which fills me with inexpressible concern, and this concern is greatly aggravated and increased when I reflect upon the uneasiness I know it will give you. It has been determined in Congress that the whole army raised for the defense of the American cause shall be put under my care, and that it is necessary for me to proceed immediately to Boston to take upon me the command of it.

You may believe me, my dear Patsy, when I assure you, in the most solemn manner, that, so far from seeking this appointment, I have used

[1] A letter written in Philadelphia on June 18, 1775, three days after his appointment.

every endeavor in my power to avoid it, not only from my unwillingness to part with you and the family, but from a consciousness of its being a trust too great for my capacity, and that I should enjoy more real happiness in one month with you at home than I have the most distant prospect of finding abroad, if my stay were to be seven times seven years. But as it has been a kind of destiny that has thrown me upon this service, I shall hope that my undertaking it is designed to answer some good purpose.

You might, and I suppose did perceive, from the tenor of my letters, that I was apprehensive I could not avoid this appointment, as I did not pretend to intimate when I should return. That was the case. It was utterly out of my power to refuse this appointment without exposing my character to such censures as would have reflected dishonor upon myself, and given pain to my friends. This, I am sure, could not, and ought not, to be pleasing to you, and must have lessened me considerably in my own esteem. I shall rely, therefore, confidently on that Providence which has heretofore preserved and been bountiful to me, not doubting but that I shall return safe to you in the fall. I shall feel no pain from the toil or the danger of the campaign; my unhappiness will flow from the uneasiness I know you will feel from being left alone. I therefore beg that you will summon your whole fortitude, and pass your time as agreeably as possible. Nothing will give me so much sincere satisfaction as to hear this, and to hear it from your own pen. My earnest and ardent desire is that you would pursue any plan that is most likely to produce content, and a tolerable degree of tranquillity; as it must add greatly to my uneasy feelings to hear that you are dissatisfied or complaining at what I really could not avoid.

As life is always uncertain, and common prudence dictates to every man the necessity of settling his temporal concerns, while it is in his power, and while the mind is calm and undisturbed, I have, since I came to this place (for I had not time to do it before I left home) got Colonel Pendleton to draft a will for me, by the directions I gave him, which will I now enclose. The provision made for you in case of my death will, I hope, be agreeable.

I shall add nothing more, as I have several letters to write, but to desire that you will remember me to your friends, and to assure you that I am with the most unfeigned regard, my dear Patsy, your affectionate, etc.

II

OF HIS ARMY IN CAMBRIDGE [2]

NOTHING would give me more real satisfaction than to know the sentiments which are entertained of me by the public, whether they be favorable or otherwise; and I urged as a reason

[2] From the letter addrest to Joseph Reed, and dated February 10, 1776. Washington had assumed command in Cambridge on July 3d of the previous year. Joseph Reed was President of the Pennsylvania Provincial Congress in 1775, and afterward became Washington's secretary and aide-de-camp. This letter was in reply to two letters from Reed containing "early and regular communication of what is passing in your quarter."

that the man who wished to steer clear of shelves and rocks must know where they lie. I know the integrity of my own heart, but to declare it, unless to a friend, may be an argument of vanity; I know the unhappy predicament I stand in: I know that much is expected of me; I know that without men, without arms, without ammunition, without anything fit for the accommodation of a soldier, little is to be done; and, what is mortifying, I know that I can not stand justified to the world without exposing my own weakness, and injuring the cause by declaring my wants, which I am determined not to do, further than unavoidable necessity brings every man acquainted with them.

If, under these disadvantages, I am able to keep above water, in the esteem of mankind, I shall feel myself happy; but if, from the unknown peculiarity of my circumstances, I suffer in the opinion of the world, I shall not think you take the freedom of a friend, if you conceal the reflections that may be cast upon my conduct. My own situation is so irksome to me at times that, if I did not consult the public good more than my own tranquillity, I should long ere this have put everything on the cast of a die. So far from my having an army of twenty thousand men well armed, I have been here with less than one-half of that number, including sick, furloughed, and on command, and those neither armed nor clothed, as they should be. In short, my situation has been such, that I have been obliged to use art to conceal it from my own officers.

The party sent to Bunker Hill had some good and some bad men engaged in it. One or two

GEORGE WASHINGTON

courts have been held on the conduct of part of them. To be plain, these people are not to be depended upon if exposed; and any man will fight well if he thinks himself in no danger. I do not apply this only to these people. I suppose it to be the case with all raw and undisciplined troops. You may rely upon it that transports left Boston six weeks ago with troops; where they are gone, unless driven to the West Indies, I know not. You may also rely upon General Clinton's sailing from Boston about three weeks ago, with about four or five hundred men; his destination I am also a stranger to. I am sorry to hear of the failures you speak of from France. But why will not Congress forward part of the powder made in your province? They seem to look upon this as the season for action, but will not furnish the means. I will not blame them. I dare say the demands upon them are greater than they can supply. The cause must be starved till our resources are greater, or more certain within ourselves.

With respect to myself, I have never entertained an idea of an accommodation since I heard of the measures which were adopted in consequence of the Bunker Hill fight. The King's speech has confirmed the sentiments I entertained upon the news of that affair; and, if every man was of my mind, the ministers of Great Britain should know, in a few words, upon what issue the cause should be put. I would not be deceived by artful declarations, nor specious pretenses; nor would I be amused by unmeaning propositions; but in open, undisguised, and manly terms proclaim our wrongs, and our resolution to be redressed. I would tell them, that we had borne much, that we had long and ardently sought for reconciliation upon honorable terms, that it had been denied us, that all our attempts after peace had proved abortive, and had been grossly misrepresented, that we had done everything which could be expected from the best of subjects, that the spirit of freedom rises too high in us to submit to slavery, and that, if nothing else would satisfy a tyrant and his diabolical ministry, we are determined to shake off all connections with a state so unjust and unnatural. This I would tell them, not under covert, but in words as clear as the sun in its meridian brightness.

III

TO THE MARQUIS DE CHASTELLUX ON HIS MARRIAGE [3]

My dear Marquis: In reading your very friendly and acceptable letter, which came to hand by the last mail, I was, as you may well suppose, not less delighted than surprized to meet the plain American words, "my wife." A wife! Well, my dear Marquis, I can hardly refrain from smiling to find you are caught at last. I saw by the eulogium you often made on the happiness of domestic life in America, that

[3] From a letter, written at Mount Vernon on April 25, 1788, and addrest to the Marquis de Chastellux, author of "Travels in North America," and a major-general in the army of Rochambeau, who served under Washington in the American Revolution.

you had swallowed the bait, and that you would as surely be taken, one day or another, as that you were a philosopher and a soldier.

So your day has at length come. I am glad of it, with all my heart and soul. It is quite good enough for you. Now you are well served for coming to fight in favor of the American rebels, all the way across the Atlantic Ocean, by catching that terrible contagion, domestic felicity, which, like the smallpox or the plague, a man can have only once in his life, because it commonly lasts him (at least with us in America; I know not how you manage these matters in France), for his whole lifetime. And yet, after all, the worst wish which I can find in my heart to make against Madame de Chastellux and yourself is that you may neither of you ever get the better of this same domestic felicity, during the entire course of your mortal existence.

If so wonderful an event should have occasioned me, my dear Marquis, to write in a strange style, you will understand me as clearly as if I had said, what in plain English is the simple truth, "Do me the justice to believe that I take a heartfelt interest in whatsoever concerns your happiness." And, in this view, I sincerely congratulate you on your auspicious matrimonial connection. I am happy to find that Madame de Chastellux is so intimately connected with the Duchess of Orleans; as I have always understood that this noble lady was an illustrious example of connubial love, as well as an excellent pattern of virtue in general.

While you have been making love under the banner of Hymen, the great personages in the north have been making war under the inspiration, or rather under the infatuation, of Mars. Now, for my part, I humbly conceive that you have acted much the best and wisest part; for certainly it is more consonant to all the principles of reason and religion, natural and revealed, to replenish the earth with inhabitants than to depopulate it by killing those already in existence. Besides, it is time for the age of knight-errantry and mad heroism to be at an end. Your young military men, who want to reap the harvest of laurels, do not care, I suppose, how many seeds of war are sown; but for the sake of humanity it is devoutly to be wished, that the manly employment of agriculture, and the humanizing benefits of commerce, would supersede the waste of war and the rage of conquest; that the swords might be turned into plowshares, the spears into pruning-hooks, and, as the Scriptures express it, the "nations learn war no more."

Now I will give you a little news from this side of the water, and then finish. As for us, we are plodding on in the dull road of peace and politics. We, who live in these ends of the earth, only hear of the rumors of war like the roar of distant thunder. It is to be hoped that our remote local situation will prevent us from being swept into its vortex.

JOHN ADAMS

Born in 1735, died in 1826; second President of the United States; graduated from Harvard in 1755; active in opposing the Stamp Act; elected to the Revolutionary Congress of Massachusetts in 1774; delegate to the first and second Continental Congresses; proposed Washington as commander-in-chief; signed the Declaration of Independence; commissioner to France in 1777; to the Netherlands in 1782, to Great Britain in 1782-83, and to Prussia; minister to England in 1785; vice-president in 1789; elected President in 1796; unsuccessful candidate for President in 1800; his "Life and Works" in ten volumes published in 1850-56.

I

ON HIS NOMINATION OF WASHINGTON TO BE COMMANDER-IN-CHIEF[1]

When Congress had assembled, I rose in my place, and in as short a speech as the subject would admit, represented the state of the colonies, the uncertainty in the minds of the people, their great expectation and anxiety, the distresses of the army, the danger of its dissolution, the difficulty of collecting another, and the probability that the British army would take advantage

[1] From the "Diary," printed in the "Works of John Adams," as edited by Charles Francis Adams. In his speech naming Washington, Adams referred to him as "one who could unite the cordial exertions of all the colonies better than any other person." Two days later he wrote to his wife that Congress had chosen "the modest and virtuous, the amiable, generous and brave George Washington, Esq., to be chief of the American army."

of our delays, march out of Boston, and spread desolation as far as they could go. I concluded with a motion, in form, that Congress would adopt the army at Cambridge, and appoint a general; that tho this was not the proper time to nominate a general, yet, as I had reason to believe, this was a point of the greatest difficulty. I had no hesitation to declare that I had but one gentleman in my mind for that important command, and that was a gentleman from Virginia who was among us and very well known to all of us, a gentleman whose skill and experience as an officer, whose independent fortune, great talents, and excellent universal character, would command the approbation of all America, and unite the cordial exertions of all the colonies better than any other person in the Union. Mr. Washington, who happened to sit near the door, as soon as he heard me allude to him, from his usual modesty, darted into the library-room. Mr. Hancock—who was our President, which gave me an opportunity to observe his countenance while I was speaking on the state of the colonies, the army at Cambridge, and the enemy—heard me with visible pleasure; but when I came to describe Washington for the commander, I never remarked a more sudden and striking change of countenance. Mortification and resentment were exprest as forcibly as his face could exhibit them. Mr. Samuel Adams seconded the motion, and that did not soften the President's physiognomy at all.

The subject came under debate, and several gentlemen declared themselves against the appointment of Mr. Washington, not on account of any personal objection against him, but be-

JOHN ADAMS

cause the army were all from New England, had a general of their own, appeared to be satisfied with him, and had proved themselves able to imprison the British army in Boston, which was all they expected or desired at that time. Mr. Pendleton, of Virginia, Mr. Sherman, of Connecticut, were very explicit in declaring this opinion; Mr. Cushing and several others more faintly exprest their opposition, and their fears of discontents in the army and in New England. Mr. Paine exprest a great opinion of General Ward and a strong friendship for him, having been his classmate at college, or at least his contemporary; but gave no opinion upon the question. The subject was postponed to a future day. In the mean time, pains were taken out-of-doors to obtain a unanimity, and the voices were generally so clearly in favor of Washington, that the dissentient members were persuaded to withdraw their opposition, and Mr. Washington was nominated, I believe by Mr. Thomas Johnson of Maryland, unanimously elected, and the army adopted.

II

AN ESTIMATE OF FRANKLIN[2]

His reputation was more universal than that of Leibnitz or Newton, Frederick or Voltaire, and his character more beloved and esteemed than any or all of them. Newton had astonished perhaps forty or fifty men in Europe, for not more than that number probably at any one time had read him and understood him, by his discoveries and demonstrations. And these being held in admiration in their respective countries, as at the head of the philosophers, had spread among scientific people a mysterious wonder at the genius of this, perhaps, the greatest man that ever lived. But this fame was confined to men of letters. The common people knew little and cared nothing about such a recluse philosopher. Leibnitz's name was more confined still. Frederick was hated by more than half of Europe as much as Louis XIV was and Napoleon is. Voltaire, whose name was more universal than any of these before mentioned, was con-

[2] From a letter to the Boston *Patriot* of May 15, 1811, now given as an appendix to the "Works of John Adams." The differences of Adams and Franklin form a striking incident in the biographies of the two men. Colaborers as they were in a common cause, they had constant disagreements as to methods while serving their country in Europe. That they never openly quarreled Adams's biographer, John T. Morse, attributes to "their sense of propriety and dignity, and to the age and position of Dr. Franklin." The radical cause lay in the fact that "they were utterly incompatible, both mentally and morally."

JOHN ADAMS

sidered as a vain, profligate wit, and not much esteemed or beloved by anybody, tho admired by all who knew his works. But Franklin's fame was universal. His name was familiar to governments and people, to kings, courtiers, nobility, clergy and philosophers, as well as plebeians, to such a degree that there was scarcely a peasant or citizen, a valet de chambre, coachman, or footman, a lady's maid, or a scullion in a kitchen, who was not familiar with it, and who did not consider him a friend to human kind. When they spoke of him they seemed to think he was to restore the Golden Age. . . .

Nothing perhaps that ever occurred upon this earth was so well calculated to give any man an extensive and universal celebrity as the discovery of the efficacy of iron points and the invention of lightning-rods. The idea was one of the most sublime that ever entered a human imagination that a mortal should disarm the clouds of heaven and almost "snatch from his hand the scepter and the rod." The ancients would have enrolled him with Bacchus and Ceres, Hercules and Minerva. . . .

Franklin had a great genius, original, sagacious, and inventive, capable of discoveries in science no less than of improvements in the fine arts and the mechanic arts. He had a vast imagination, equal to the comprehension of the greatest objects, and capable of a steady and cool comprehension of them. He had wit at will. He had humor that, when he pleased, was delicate and delightful. He had a satire that was good-natured or caustic, Horace or Juvenal, Swift or Rabelais, at his pleasure. He had talents for irony, allegory, and fable, that he could adapt with great skill to the promotion of moral and political truth. He was master of that infantine simplicity which the French call *naïveté,* which never fails to charm, in Phædrus and La Fontaine, from the cradle to the grave.

Had he been blest with the same advantages of scholastic education in his early youth, and pursued a course of studies as unembarrassed with occupations of public and private life, as Sir Isaac Newton, he might have emulated the first philosopher. Altho I am not ignorant that most of his positions and hypotheses have been controverted, I can not but think he has added much to the mass of natural knowledge, and contributed largely to the progress of the human mind, both by his own writings and by the controversies and experiments he has excited in all parts of Europe. He had abilities for investigating statistical questions, and in some parts of his life has written pamphlets and essays upon public topics with great ingenuity and success; but after my acquaintance with him, which commenced in Congress in 1775, his excellence as a legislator, a politician, or a negotiator most certainly never appeared. No sentiments more weak and superficial were ever avowed by the most absurd philosopher than some of his, particularly one that he procured to be inserted in the first constitution of Pennsylvania, and for which he had such a fondness as to insert it in his will. I call it weak, for so it must have been, or hypocritical; unless he meant by one satiric touch to ridicule his own republic, or throw it into everlasting contempt.

JOHN ADAMS

I must acknowledge, after all, that nothing in life has mortified or grieved me more than the necessity which compelled me to oppose him so often as I have. He was a man with whom I always wished to live in friendship, and for that purpose omitted no demonstration of respect, esteem, and veneration in my power, until I had unequivocal proofs of his hatred, for no other reason under the sun, but because I gave my judgment in opposition to his, in many points which materially affected the interests of our country, and in many more which essentially concerned our happiness, safety, and well-being. I could not and would not sacrifice the clearest dictates of my understanding and the purest principles of morals and policy in compliance to Dr. Franklin.

THOMAS PAINE

Born in England in 1737, died in New York in 1809; came to America in 1774; took a prominent part in the Revolution as a writer; his "Common Sense," advocating independence, published in 1776; published a periodical, *The Crisis*, in 1776-83; went to Europe in 1787; in 1792 was outlawed from England for publishing his "Rights of Man"; went to France and elected to the National Convention in 1793; imprisoned in France in 1794; published his "Age of Reason" in 1794; returned to the United States in 1802.

IN FAVOR OF SEPARATION OF THE COLONIES FROM GREAT BRITAIN[1]

THE blood of the slain, the weeping voice of nature cries, "'tis time to part." Even the distance at which the Almighty hath placed England and America, is a strong and natural proof that the authority of the one over the other was never the design of heaven. The time, likewise, at which the continent was discovered, adds weight to the argument, and the manner in which it was peopled, increases the force of it. The Reformation was preceded by the discovery of

[1] From "Common Sense," a pamphlet issued by Paine in Philadelphia on January 1, 1776. In this work Paine advocated complete separation from England. His arguments helped to consolidate and make effective a sentiment which already was drifting in the same direction. Washington said he effected "a powerful change in the minds of many men."

THOMAS PAINE

America, as if the Almighty graciously meant to open a sanctuary to the persecuted in future years, when home should afford neither friendship nor safety.

The authority of Great Britain over this continent is a form of government which sooner or later must have an end: and a serious mind can draw no true pleasure by looking forward, under the painful and positive conviction that what he calls "the present constitution" is merely temporary. As parents, we can have no joy knowing that this government is not sufficiently lasting to insure anything which we may bequeath to posterity; and by a plain method of argument, as we are running the next generation into debt, we ought to do the work of it, otherwise we use them meanly and pitifully. In order to discover the line of our duty rightly, we should take our children in our hand, and fix our station a few years farther into life; that eminence will present a prospect which a few present fears and prejudices conceal from our sight.

Tho I would carefully avoid giving unnecessary offense, yet I am inclined to believe that all those who espouse the doctrine of reconciliation may be included within the following descriptions:

Interested men, who are not to be trusted; weak men, who can not see; prejudiced men, who will not see; and a certain set of moderate men, who think better of the European world than it deserves: and this last class, by an ill-judged deliberation, will be the cause of more calamities to this continent than all the other three.

It is the good fortune of many to live distant from the scene of sorrow; the evil is not sufficiently brought to their doors to make them feel the precariousness with which all American property is possest. But let our imaginations transport us a few moments to Boston; that seat of wretchedness will teach us wisdom, and instruct us forever to renounce a power in whom we can have no trust. The inhabitants of that unfortunate city, who but a few months ago were in ease and affluence, have now no other alternative than to stay and starve, or turn out to beg. Endangered by the fire of their friends if they continue within the city, and plundered by the soldiery if they leave it. In their present situation they are prisoners without the hope of redemption, and in a general attack for their relief they would be exposed to the fury of both armies.

Men of passive tempers look somewhat lightly over the offenses of Britain, and, still hoping for the best, are apt to call out, "Come, come, we shall be friends again for all this." But examine the passions and feelings of mankind, bring the doctrine of reconciliation to the touchstone of nature, and then tell me whether you can hereafter love, honor, and faithfully serve the power that hath carried fire and sword into your land? If you can not do all these, then are you only deceiving yourselves, and by your delay bringing ruin upon your posterity. Your future connection with Britain, whom you can neither love nor honor, will be forced and unnatural, and being formed only on the plan of present convenience, will in a little time fall into a relapse more wretched than the first. But if you say

THOMAS PAINE

you can still pass the violations over, then I ask, hath your house been burnt? Hath your property been destroyed before your face? Are your wife and children destitute of a bed to lie on, or bread to live on? Have you lost a parent or a child by their hands, and yourself the ruined and wretched survivor? If you have not, then are you not a judge of those who have. But if you have, and can still shake hands with the murderers, then are you unworthy the name of husband, father, friend, or lover, and, whatever may be your rank or title in life, you have the heart of a coward and the spirit of a sycophant.

THOMAS JEFFERSON

Born in 1743, died in 1826; Member of the Virginia House of Burgesses in 1769-75, and again in 1776-78; Member of the Continental Congress in 1775; drafted the Declaration of Independence in 1776; Governor of Virginia in 1779; Member of Congress in 1783; Minister to France in 1785; Secretary of State in 1790; Vice-President in 1797; elected President in 1801 and reelected in 1805.

I

WHEN THE BASTILE FELL[1]

IN the meantime these troops, to the number of twenty to thirty thousand, had arrived and were posted in and between Paris and Versailles. The bridges and passes were guarded. The King was now completely in the hands of men the principal among whom had been noted, through their lives, for the Turkish despotism of their characters, and who were associated around the King as proper instruments for what was to be executed. The news of this change began to be known at Paris about one or two o'clock. In the afternoon a body of about one hundred German cavalry were advanced, and drawn up in the Place Louis XV, and about two hundred Swiss posted at a little distance in their rear. This drew people to the spot, who thus

[1] From the "Autobiography," now printed in Volume I of the "Writings of Jefferson," edited by Paul Leicester Ford.

accidentally found themselves in front of the troops, merely at first as spectators; but, as their numbers increased, their indignation rose. They retired a few steps, and posted themselves on and behind large piles of stones, large and small, collected in that place for a bridge, which was to be built adjacent to it.

In this position, happening to be in my carriage on a visit, I passed through the lane they had formed without interruption. But the moment after I had passed, the people attacked the cavalry with stones. They charged, but the advantageous position of the people, and the showers of stones, obliged the horse to retire, and quit the field altogether, leaving one of their number on the ground, and the Swiss in the rear not moving to their aid. This was the signal for universal insurrection, and this body of cavalry, to avoid being massacred, retired toward Versailles. The people now armed themselves with such weapons as they could find in armorers' shops, and private houses, and with bludgeons; and were roaming all night, through all parts of the city, without any decided object.

The next day (the 13th) the Assembly prest on the King to send away the troops, to permit the bourgeoisie of Paris to arm for the preservation of order in the city, and offered to send a deputation from their body to tranquillize them; but their propositions were refused. A committee of magistrates and electors of the city were appointed by those bodies, to take upon them its government. The people, now openly joined by the French guards, forced the prison of St. Lazare, released all the prisoners, and took a great store of corn, which they carried to the corn-market. Here they got some arms, and the French guards began to form and train them. The city committee determined to raise forty-eight thousand bourgeoisie, or rather to restrain their numbers to forty-eight thousand.

On the 14th, they sent one of their members (Monsieur de Corny) to the Hotel des Invalides, to ask arms for their Garde Bourgeoisie. He was followed by, and he found there, a great collection of people. The Governor of the Invalids came out, and represented the impossibility of his delivering arms without the orders of those from whom he received them. De Corny advised the people then to retire, and retired himself; but the people took possession of the arms. It was remarkable that not only the Invalids themselves made no opposition, but that a body of five thousand foreign troops, within four hundred yards, never stirred. M. De Corny, and five others, were then sent to ask arms of M. de Launay, Governor of the Bastile. They found a great collection of people already before the place, and they immediately planted a flag of truce, which was answered by a like flag hoisted on the parapet. The deputation prevailed on the people to fall back a little, advanced themselves to make their demand of the Governor, and in that instant a discharge from the Bastile killed four persons of those nearest to the deputies. The deputies retired. I happened to be at the house of M. de Corny, when he returned to it, and received from him a narrative of these transactions.

On the retirement of the deputies the people

rushed forward, and almost in an instant were in possession of a fortification of infinite strength, defended by one hundred men, which in other times had stood several regular sieges, and had never been taken. How they forced their entrance has never been explained. They took all the arms, discharged the prisoners, and such of the garrison as were not killed in the first moment of fury; carried the Governor and Lieutenant-Governor to the Place de Grève (the place of public execution), cut off their heads, and sent them through the city, in triumph, to the Palais royal. About the same instant a treacherous correspondence having been discovered in M. de Flesseles, Prevôt des Marchands, they seized him in the Hotel de Ville, where he was in the execution of his office, and cut off his head.

These events, carried imperfectly to Versailles, were the subject of two successive deputations from the Assembly to the King, to both of which he gave dry and hard answers; for nobody had as yet been permitted to inform him, truly and fully, of what had passed at Paris. But at night the Duke de Liancourt forced his way into the King's bedchamber, and obliged him to hear a full and animated detail of the disasters of the day in Paris. He went to bed fearfully imprest. The decapitation of de Launay worked powerfully through the night on the whole Aristocratic party; insomuch that in the morning those of the greatest influence on the Count d'Artois represented to him the absolute necessity that the King should give up everything to the Assembly. This according with the dispositions of the King, he went about eleven o'clock, accompanied only by his brothers, to the Assembly, and there read to them a speech, in which he asked their interposition to reestablish order. Altho couched in terms of some caution, yet the manner in which it was delivered made it evident that it was meant as a surrender at discretion. He returned to the Chateau afoot, accompanied by the Assembly.

They sent off a deputation to quiet Paris, at the head of which was the Marquis de La Fayette, who had, the same morning, been named Commandant en chef of the Milice Bourgeoise; and Monsieur Bailly, former President of the States General, was called for as Prevôt des Marchands. The demolition of the Bastile was now ordered and begun. A body of the Swiss guards, of the regiment of Ventimille, and the city horse guards joined the people. The alarm at Versailles increased. The foreign troops were ordered off instantly. Every minister resigned. The King confirmed Bailly as Prevôt des Marchands, wrote to M. Necker, to recall him, sent his letter open to the Assembly, to be forwarded by them, and invited them to go with him to Paris the next day, to satisfy the city of his dispositions; and that night, and the next morning, the Count d'Artois, and M. de Montesson, a deputy connected with him, Madame de Polignac, Madame de Guiche, and the Count de Vaudreuil, favorites of the Queen, the Abbe de Vermont, her confessor, the Prince of Conde, and the Duke of Bourbon fled.

The King came to Paris, leaving the Queen in consternation for his return. Omitting the less important figures of the procession, the

THOMAS JEFFERSON

King's carriage was in the center; on each side of it the Assembly, in two ranks afoot; at their head the Marquis de La Fayette, as Commander-in-chief, on horseback, and Bourgeois guards before and behind. About sixty thousand citizens, of all forms and conditions, armed with the conquests of the Bastile and Invalids, as far as they would go, the rest with pistols, swords, pikes, pruning-hooks, scythes, etc., lined all the streets through which the procession passed, and with the crowds of people in the streets, doors, and windows, saluted them everywhere with the cries of "vive la nation," but not a single "vive le roi" was heard. The King stopt at the Hotel de Ville. There M. Bailly presented, and put into his hat the popular cockade, and addrest him. The King being unprepared, and unable to answer, Bailly went to him, gathered from him some scraps of sentences, and made out an answer, which he delivered to the audience as from the King. On their return, the popular cries were "vive le Roi et la nation." He was conducted by a Garde Bourgeoise to his palace at Versailles, and thus concluded an "amende honorable," as no sovereign ever made, and no people ever received.

And here, again, was lost another precious occasion of sparing to France the crimes and cruelties through which she has since passed, and to Europe, and finally America, the evils which flowed on them also from this mortal source. The King was now become a passive machine in the hands of the National Assembly, and had he been left to himself, he would have willingly acquiesced in whatever they should devise as best for the nation. A wise constitution would have been formed, hereditary in his line, himself placed at its head, with powers so large as to enable him to do all the good of his station, and so limited as to restrain him from its abuse. This he would have faithfully administered, and more than this I do not believe he ever wished. But he had a Queen of absolute sway over his weak mind and timid virtue, and of a character the reverse of his in all points. This angel, as gaudily painted in the rhapsodies of Burke,[2] with some smartness of fancy, but no sound sense, was proud, disdainful of restraint, indignant at all obstacles to her will, eager in the pursuit of pleasure, and firm enough to hold to her desires, or perish in their wreck. Her inordinate gambling and dissipations, with those of the Count d'Artois, and others of her *clique*, had been a sensible item in the exhaustion of the treasury, which called into action the reforming hand of the nation; and her opposition to it, her inflexible perverseness, and dauntless spirit, led herself to the guillotine, drew the King on with her, and plunged the world into crimes and calamities which will forever stain the pages of modern history.

I have ever believed that had there been no Queen there would have been no revolution. No force would have been provoked, nor exercised. The King would have gone hand in hand with the wisdom of his sounder counselors, who, guided by the increased lights of the age, wished only, with the same pace, to advance the principles

[2] See page 214 of Volume IV of this collection for this tribute from Burke.

THOMAS JEFFERSON

of their social constitution. The deed which closed the mortal course of these sovereigns I shall neither approve nor condemn. I am not perpared to say that the first magistrate of a nation can not commit treason against his country, or is unamenable to its punishment; nor yet that where there is no written law, no regulated tribunal, there is not a law in our hearts, and a power in our hands, given for righteous employment in maintaining right and redressing wrong. Of those who judged the King many thought him wilfully criminal; many, that his existence would keep the nation in perpetual conflict with the horde of kings who would war against a generation which might come home to themselves, and that it were better that one should die than all. I should not have voted with this portion of the Legislature. I should have shut up the Queen in a convent, putting harm out of her power, and placed the King in his station, investing him with limited powers, which, I verily believe, he would have honestly exercised, according to the measure of his understanding. In this way no void would have been created, courting the usurpation of a military adventurer, nor occasion given for those enormities which demoralized the nations of the world, and destroyed, and are yet to destroy millions and millions of its inhabitants.

II

THE FUTILITY OF DISPUTES[3]

I HAVE mentioned good humor as one of the preservatives of our peace and tranquillity. It is among the most effectual, and its effect is so well imitated and aided, artificially, by politeness that this also becomes an acquisition of first-rate value. In truth, politeness is artificial good humor; it covers the natural want of it, and ends by rendering habitual a substitute nearly equivalent to the real virtue. It is the practise of sacrificing to those whom we meet in society all the little conveniences and preferences which will gratify them, and deprive us of nothing worth a moment's consideration; it is the giving a pleasing and flattering turn to our expressions, which will conciliate others, and make them pleased with us as well as themselves. How cheap a price for the good will of another! When this is in return for a rude thing said by another, it brings him to his senses, it mortifies and corrects him in the most salutary way, and places him at the feet of your good nature in the eyes of the company.

But in stating prudential rules for our government in society I must not omit the important one of never entering into dispute or argument with another. I never saw an instance of one of two disputants convincing the other by argu-

[3] From a letter to Thomas Jefferson Randolph, dated Washington, Nov. 24, 1808.

THOMAS JEFFERSON

ment. I have seen many, on their getting warm, becoming rude, and shooting one another. Conviction is the effect of our own dispassionate reasoning, either in solitude, or weighing within ourselves, dispassionately, what we hear from others, standing uncommitted in argument ourselves. It was one of the rules which, above all others, made Doctor Franklin the most amiable of men in society "never to contradict anybody." If he was urged to announce an opinion, he did it rather by asking questions, as if for information, or by suggesting doubts. When I hear another express an opinion which is not mine, I say to myself he has a right to his opinion, as I to mine; why should I question it? His error does me no injury, and shall I become a Don Quixote, to bring all men by force of argument to one opinion? If a fact be misstated, it is probable he is gratified by a belief of it, and I have no right to deprive him of the gratification. If he wants information, he will ask it, and then I will give it in measured terms; but if he still believes his own story, and shows a desire to dispute the fact with me, I hear him and say nothing. It is his affair, not mine, if he prefers error.

There are two classes of disputants most frequently to be met with among us. The first is of young students, just entered the threshold of science, with a first view of its outlines, not yet filled up with the details and modifications which a further progress would bring to their knowledge. The other consists of the ill-tempered and rude men in society, who have taken up a passion for politics. (Good humor and politeness never introduce into mixt society a question on which they foresee there will be a difference of opinion.) From both of those classes of disputants, my dear Jefferson, keep aloof as you would from the infected subjects of yellow fever or pestilence. Consider yourself, when with them, as among the patients of Bedlam, needing medical more than moral counsel. Be a listener only, keep within yourself, and endeavor to establish with yourself the habit of silence, especially on politics. In the fevered state of our country no good can ever result from any attempt to set one of these fiery zealots to rights, either in fact or principle. They are determined as to the facts they will believe, and the opinions on which they will act. Get by them, therefore, as you would by an angry bull; it is not for a man of sense to dispute the road with such an animal.

III

OF BLACKS AND WHITES IN THE SOUTH [4]

It will probably be asked, Why not retain and incorporate the blacks into the state, and thus save the expense of supplying by importation of white settlers the vacancies they will leave? Deep-rooted prejudices entertained by the

[4] From Query No. 14 of the "Notes on the State of Virginia," which, says Jefferson in an "advertisement," "were written in Virginia in the year 1781 and somewhat corrected and enlarged in the winter of 1782, in answer to queries proposed to the author by a foreigner of distinction then residing among us."

whites; ten thousand recollections, by the blacks, of the injuries they have sustained; new provocations; the real distinctions which nature has made; and many other circumstances will divide us into parties, and produce convulsions which will probably never end but in the extermination of the one or the other race. To these objections, which are political, may be added others, which are physical and moral.

The first difference which strikes us is that of color. Whether the black of the negro resides in the reticular membrane between the skin and the scarf-skin, or in the scarf-skin itself; whether it proceeds from the color of the blood, the color of the bile, or from that of some other secretion, the difference is fixt in nature, and is as real as if its seat and cause were better known to us. And is this difference of no importance? Is it not the foundation of a greater or less share of beauty in the two races? Are not the fine mixtures of red and white, the expressions of every passion by greater or less suffusions of color in the one, preferable to that eternal monotony which reigns in the countenances, that immovable veil of black which covers all the emotions of the other race?

Add to these flowing hair, a more elegant symmetry of form, their own judgment in favor of the whites, declared by their preference of them, as uniformly as is the preference of the orang-utan for the black women over those of his own species. The circumstance of superior beauty is thought worthy attention in the propagation of our horses, dogs, and other domestic animals; why not in that of man? Besides those of color, figure, and hair, there are other physical distinctions proving a difference of race. They have less hair on the face and body. They secrete less by the kidneys, and more by the glands of the skin, which gives them a very strong and disagreeable odor. This great degree of transpiration renders them more tolerant of heat, and less so of cold than the whites.

Perhaps, too, a difference of structure in the pulmonary apparatus, which a late ingenious experimentalist has discovered to be the principal regulator of animal heat, may have disabled them from extricating, in the act of inspiration, so much of that fluid from the outer air, or obliged them in expiration to part with more of it. They seem to require less sleep. A black, after hard labor through the day, will be induced by the slightest amusement to sit up till midnight, or later, tho knowing he must be out with the first dawn of the morning. They are at least as brave, and more adventuresome.

But this may perhaps proceed from a want of forethought, which prevents their seeing a danger till it be present. When present, they do not go through it with more coolness or steadiness than the whites. They are more ardent after their female; but love seems with them to be more an eager desire than a tender, delicate mixture of sentiment and sensation. Their griefs are transient. Those numberless afflictions, which render it doubtful whether heaven has given life to us in mercy or in wrath, are less felt, and sooner forgotten with them. In general, their existence appears to participate more of sensation than reflection. To this must be ascribed their disposition to sleep when abstracted from their diversions, and unemployed in labor. An animal, whose body is at rest and who does not reflect, must be disposed to sleep, of course. Comparing them by their faculties of memory, reason, and imagination, it appears to me that in memory they are equal to the whites; in reason much inferior, as I think one could scarcely be found capable of tracing and comprehending the investigations of Euclid; and that in imagination they are dull, tasteless, and anomalous.

It would be unfair to follow them to Africa for this investigation. We will consider them here, on the same stage with the whites, and where the facts are not apocryphal on which a judgment is to be formed. It will be right to make great allowances for the difference of condition, of education, of conversation, of the sphere in which they move. Many millions of them have been brought to, and born in America. Most of them, indeed, have been confined to tillage, to their own homes, and their own society; yet many have been so situated that they might have availed themselves of the conversation of their masters; many have been brought up to the handicraft arts, and from that circumstance have always been associated with the white. Some have been liberally educated, and all have lived in countries where the arts and sciences are cultivated to a considerable degree, and have had before their eyes samples of the best works from abroad.

The Indians, with no advantages of their kind, will often carve figures on their pipes not destitute of design and merit. They will crayon out an animal, a plant, or a country, so as to prove the existence of a germ in their minds which only wants cultivation. They astonish you with strokes of the most sublime oratory; such as prove their reason and sentiment strong, their imagination glowing and elevated. But never yet could I find that a black had uttered a thought above the level of plain narration; never saw even an elementary trait of painting or sculpture. In music they are more generally gifted than the whites with accurate ears for tune and time, and they have been found capable of imagining a small catch. Whether they will be equal to the composition of a more extensive run of melody, or of complicated harmony is yet to be proved. Misery is often the parent of the most affecting touches in poetry. Among the blacks is misery enough, God knows, but no poetry. Love is the peculiar œstrum of the poet. Their love is ardent, but it kindles the senses only, not the imagination. . . .

There must doubtless be an unhappy influence on the manners of our people produced by the existence of slavery among us. The whole commerce between master and slave is a perpetual exercise of the most boisterous passions — the most unremitting despotism on the one part and degrading submissions on the other. Our children see this, and learn to imitate it; for man is an imitative animal. This quality is the germ of all education in him. From his cradle to his grave he is learning to do what he sees others do. If a parent could find no motive either in his philanthropy or his self-love for restraining the intemperance of passion toward his slave, it should always be a sufficient one that his child is present.

But generally it is not sufficient. The parent storms; the child looks on, catches the lineaments of wrath, puts on the same airs, in the circle of smaller slaves gives a loose to the worst of passions, and thus nursed, educated, and daily exercised in tyranny, can not but be stamped by it with odious peculiarities. The man must be a prodigy who can retain his manners and morals undepraved by such circumstances. And with what execrations should the statesman be loaded who, permitting one-half the citizens thus to trample on the rights of the other, transforms those into despots and these into enemies, destroys the morals of the one part and the *amor patriæ* of the other! For if a slave can have a country in this world, it must be any other in preference to that in which he is born to live and labor for another; in which he must lock up the faculties of his nature, contribute as far as depends on his individual endeavors to the evanishment of the human race, or entail his own miserable condition on the endless generations proceeding from him. With the morals of the people, their industry is destroyed. For in a warm climate no man will labor for himself who can make another labor for him. This is so true that of the proprietors of slaves a very small proportion indeed are ever seen to labor.

IV

HIS ACCOUNT OF LOGAN'S FAMOUS SPEECH[5]

The principles of their society forbidding all compulsion, they are to be led to duty and to enterprise by personal influence and persuasion. Hence eloquence in council, bravery and success in war become the foundations of all consequence with them. To these acquirements all their faculties are directed. Of their bravery and address in war we have multiplied proofs, because we have been the subjects on which they were exercised. Of their eminence in oratory we have fewer examples, because it is displayed chiefly in their own councils. Some, however, we have of very superior luster. I may challenge the whole orations of Demosthenes and Cicero, and of any more eminent orator, if Europe has furnished any more eminent, to produce a single passage superior to the speech of Logan, a Mingo chief, to Lord Dunmore, when governor of this State. And, as a testimony of their talents in this line, I beg leave to introduce it, first stating the incidents necessary for understanding it.

In the spring of the year 1774 a robbery was committed by some Indians on certain land adventurers on the river Ohio. The whites in that quarter, according to their custom, undertook to punish this outrage in a summary way. Captain Michael Cresap, and a certain Daniel Great-

[5] From Query VI of the "Notes on Virginia."

house leading on these parties, surprized, at different times, traveling and hunting parties of the Indians, having their women and children with them, and murdered many. Among these were unfortunately the family of Logan, a chief celebrated in peace and war, and long distinguished as the friend of the whites. This unworthy return provoked his vengeance. He accordingly signalized himself in the war which ensued. In the autumn of the same year a decisive battle was fought at the mouth of the Great Kanawha, between the collected forces of the Shawanese, Mingoes and Delawares, and a detachment of the Virginia militia. The Indians were defeated and sued for peace. Logan, however, disdained to be seen among the suppliants. But lest the sincerity of a treaty should be disturbed, from which so distinguished a chief absented himself, he sent, by a messenger, the speech, to be delivered to Lord Dunmore.[6] . . .

The story of Logan is repeated precisely as it had been current for more than a dozen years before it was published. When Lord Dunmore returned from the expedition against the Indians, in 1774, he and his officers brought the speech of Logan, and related the circumstances connected with it. These were so affecting, and the speech itself so fine a morsel of eloquence, that it became the theme of every conversation, in Williamsburg particularly, and generally, indeed, wheresoever any of the officers resided or

[6] For the text of Logan's speech see Volume VIII of "The World's Famous Orations," William J. Bryan, editor-in-in-chief; Francis W. Halsey, associate editor; Funk and Wagnalls Company, publishers.

resorted. I learned it in Williamsburgh; I believe at Lord Dunmore's; and I find in my pocket-book of that year (1774) an entry of the narrative, as taken from the mouth of some person, whose name, however, is not noted, nor recollected, precisely in the words stated in the "Notes on Virginia." The speech was published in the *Virginia Gazette* of that time (I have it myself in the volume of gazettes of that year), and tho in a style by no means elegant, yet it was so admired that it flew through all the public papers of the continent, and through the magazines and other periodical publications of Great Britain; and those who were boys at that day will now attest that the speech of Logan used to be given them as a school exercise for repetition. It was not till about thirteen or fourteen years after the newspaper publications that the "Notes on Virginia" were published in America. Combating in these the contumelious theory of certain European writers, whose celebrity have currency and weight to their opinions, that our country, from the combined effects of soil and climate, degenerated animal nature, in the general, and particularly the moral faculties of man, I considered the speech of Logan as an apt proof of the contrary, and used it as such; and I copied, verbatim, the narrative I had taken down in 1774 and the speech as it had been given us in a better translation by Lord Dunmore."[7]

[7] The above final paragraph is from the appendix to the second edition of the "Notes on Virginia," and was called forth by public criticism of the statements made in the text.

GOUVERNEUR MORRIS

Born in 1752, died in 1816; member of the First and Second Continental Congresses; chairman of the committee which conferred with the British peace commissioners in 1778; drafted a scheme for a system of coinage which is the basis of our present system; member of the Convention which drafted the Constitution, taking a leading part in all the debates; went to France in 1789 on private business, and witnessed the outbreak of the Revolution; kept a diary and wrote important letters; minister to France in 1792; United States Senator from New York in 1800; active in promoting the Erie Canal project until his death; his biography written by Theodore Roosevelt; his "Diary and Letters" published in 1888.

I

THE OPENING OF THE FRENCH STATES-GENERAL[1]

I HAD the honor to be present on the fifth of this month at the opening of the States-General; a spectacle more solemn to the mind than gaudy to the eye. And yet, there was displayed everything of noble and of royal in this titled country. A great number of fine women, and a very great number of fine dresses, ranged round the hall. On a kind of stage the throne; on the left of the King and a little below him the Queen; a little behind him to the right, and on chairs, the princes

[1] From a letter written in 1789 and addrest to Mrs. Morris of Philadelphia. Copyright, 1888, by Charles Scribner's Sons.

of the blood; on the right and left, at some distance from the throne, the various princesses, with the gentlemen and ladies of their retinue. Advanced on the stage, to the left of the throne, the Keeper of the Seals. Several officers of the household, richly caparisoned, strewed about in different places. Behind the throne a cluster of guards, of the largest size, drest in ancient costumes, taken from the times of chivalry. In front of the throne on the right, below the stage, the ministers of state, with a long table before them. On the opposite side of the hall some benches, on which sat the maréchals of France, and other great officers. In front of the ministers, on benches facing the opposite side of the hall, sat the representatives of the clergy, being priests of all colors, scarlet, crimson, black, white, and gray, to the number of three hundred. In front of the maréchals of France, on benches facing the clergy, sat an equal number of representatives of the nobility, drest in a robe of black, waistcoats of cloth of gold, and over their shoulders, so as to hang forward to their waists, a kind of lapels about a quarter of a yard wide at top, and wider at bottom, made of cloth of gold. On benches, which reached quite across the hall, and facing the stage, sat the representatives of the people clothed in black. In the space between the clergy and nobles, directly in front of the representatives of the people, and facing the throne, stood the heralds-at-arms, with their staves and in very rich dresses.

When the King entered, he was saluted with a shout of applause. Some time after he had taken his seat, he put on a round beaver, ornamented with white plumes, the part in front turned up, with a large diamond button in the center. He read his speech well, and was interrupted at a part which affected his audience by a loud shout of *Vive le Roi*. After this had subsided, he finished his speech, and received again an animated acclamation of applause. He then took off his hat, and after a while put it on again, at which the nobles also put on their hats, which resembled the King's, excepting the button. The effect of this display of plumage was fine.

The Keeper of the Seals then performed his genuflexions to the throne, and mumbled out, in a very ungraceful manner, a speech of considerable length, which nobody pretends to judge of, because nobody heard it. He was succeeded by M. Necker,[2] who soon handed his speech to his clerk, being unable to go through with it. The clerk delivered it much better than the minister, and that is no great praise. It was three hours long, contained many excellent things, but too much of compliment, too much of repetition, and indeed too much of everything, for it was too long by two hours, and yet fell short in some capital points of great expectation. He received, however, very repeated plaudits from the audience, some of which were merited, but more were certainly paid to his character than to his

---

[2] Jacques Necker, director of the Treasury in 1776; resigned in 1781; recalled in 1788; convened the States-General in 1789; dismissed in the same year and again recalled, but finally resigned in 1790. Married Mlle. Susanne Curchod, Gibbon's early love, and became the father of Madame de Staël.

composition. M. Necker's long speech now comes to a close, and the King rises to depart. The hall resounds with a long loud *Vive le Roi*. He passes the Queen, who rises to follow him. At this moment some one, imbued with the milk of human kindness, originates a faint *Vive la Reine*. She makes a humble courtesy and presents the sinking of the high Austrian spirit; a livelier acclamation in return, and to this her lowlier bending, which is succeeded by a shout of loud applause. Here drops the curtain on the first great act of this great drama, in which Bourbon gives freedom. His courtiers seem to feel what he seems to be insensible of, the pang of greatness going off.

II

OF THE EXECUTION OF LOUIS XVI[3]

THE late King of this country has been publicly executed. He died in a manner becoming his dignity. Mounting the scaffold, he exprest anew his forgiveness of those who persecuted him, and a prayer that his deluded people might be benefited by his death. On the scaffold he attempted to speak, but the commanding officer, Santerre, ordered the drums to beat. The King made two unavailing efforts, but with the same bad success. The executioners threw him down,

[3] From a letter to Thomas Jefferson, dated Paris, January 25, 1793, printed in Volume II, Chapter 28, of Morris's "Diary and Letters." Copyright, 1888, by Charles Scribner's Sons.

and were in such haste as to let fall the ax before his neck was properly placed, so that he was mangled.

It would be needless to give you an affecting narrative of particulars. I proceed to what is more important, having but a few minutes to write in by the present good opportunity. The greatest care was taken to prevent a concourse of people. This proves a conviction that the majority was not favorable to that severe measure. In fact, the great mass of the people mourned the fate of their unhappy prince. I have seen grief, such as for the untimely death of a beloved parent. Everything wears an appearance of solemnity which is awfully distressing. I have been told by a gentleman from the spot that putting the King to death would be a signal for disbanding the army in Flanders. I do not believe this, but incline to think it will have some effect on the army, already perishing by want and moldering fast away. The people of that country, if the French army retreats, will, I am persuaded, take a severe vengeance for the injuries they have felt and the insults they have been exposed to. Both are great. The war against France is become popular in Austria, and is becoming so in Germany. If my judgment be good, the testament of Louis the Sixteenth will be more powerful against the present rulers of this country than any army of a hundred thousand men. You will learn the effect it has in England. I believe that the English will be wound up to a pitch of enthusiastic horror against France, which their cool and steady temper seems to be scarcely susceptible of.

I enclose you a translation of a letter from Sweden, which I have received from Denmark. You will see thereby that the Jacobin principles are propagated with zeal in every quarter. Whether the Regent of Sweden intends to make himself king is a moot point. All the world knows that the young prince is not legitimate, altho born under circumstances which render it, legally speaking, impossible to question his legitimacy. I consider a war between Britain and France is inevitable. I have not proof, but some very leading circumstances. Britain will, I think, suspend her blow until she can strike very hard, unless, indeed, they should think it advisable to seize the moment of indignation against late events for a declaration of war. This is not improbable, because it may be coupled with those general declarations against all kings, under the name of tyrants, which contain a determination to destroy them, and the threat that if the ministers of England presume to declare war, an appeal shall be made to the people at the head of an invading army. Of course, a design may be exhibited of entering into the heart of Great Britain, to overrun the Constitution, destroy the rights of property, and finally to dethrone and murder the King—all which are things the English will neither approve of nor submit to.

ALEXANDER HAMILTON

Born in 1757, died in 1804; a pamphleteer in the agitation preceding the Revolution; a captain of artillery in 1776; on Washington's staff in 1777-81: won distinction at Yorktown in 1781; member of the Continental Congress in 1782; member of the Constitutional Convention of 1787; Secretary of the Treasury in 1789; commander-in-chief of the army in 1799; killed in a duel by Aaron Burr in 1804.

I

OF THE FAILURE OF CONFEDERATION[1]

In the course of the preceding papers, I have endeavored, my fellow citizens, to place before you, in a clear and convincing light, the importance of union to your political safety and happiness. I have unfolded to you a complication of dangers to which you would be exposed, should you permit that sacred knot, which binds the people of America together, to be severed or dissolved by ambition or by avarice, by jealousy or by misrepresentation. In the sequel of the inquiry through which I propose to accompany you the truths intended to be inculcated will receive further confirmation from facts and arguments hitherto unnoticed. If the road over which you will still have to pass should in some places appear to you tedious or irksome, you will recol-

[1] From No. 15 of the "Federalist" Papers, now printed in Volume IX of the "Works of Hamilton," edited by Henry Cabot Lodge.

lect that you are in quest of information on a subject the most momentous which can engage the attention of a free people; that the field through which you have to travel is in itself spacious, and that the difficulties of the journey have been unnecessarily increased by the mazes with which sophistry has beset the way. It will be my aim to remove the obstacles to your progress in as compendious a manner as it can be done without sacrificing utility to dispatch.

In pursuance of the plan which I have laid down for the discussion of the subject, the point next in order to be examined is the "insufficiency of the present confederation to the preservation of the Union."

It may perhaps be asked what need there is of reasoning or proof to illustrate a position which is neither controverted nor doubted; to which the understandings and feelings of all classes of men assent; and which in substance is admitted by the opponents as well as by the friends of the new constitution? It must in truth be acknowledged that, however these may differ in other respects, they in general appear to harmonize in the opinion that there are material imperfections in our national system, and that something is necessary to be done to rescue us from impending anarchy. The facts that support this opinion are no longer objects of speculation. They have forced themselves upon the sensibility of the people at large, and have at length extorted from those whose mistaken policy has had the principal share in precipitating the extremity at which we are arrived, a reluctant confession of the reality of many of those defects in the scheme of our federal government which have been long pointed out and regretted by the intelligent friends of the Union.

We may, indeed, with propriety be said to have reached almost the last stage of national humiliation. There is scarcely anything that can wound the pride, or degrade the character of an independent people which we do not experience. Are there engagements, to the performance of which we are held by every tie respectable among men? These are the subjects of constant and unblushing violation. Do we owe debts to foreigners, and to our own citizens, contracted in a time of imminent peril, for the preservation of our political existence? These remain without any proper or satisfactory provision for their discharge. Have we valuable territories and important posts in the possession of a foreign power, which, by express stipulations, ought long since to have been surrendered? These are still retained, to the prejudice of our interests not less than of our rights. Are we in a condition to resent or to repel the aggression? We have neither troops, nor treasury, nor government. Are we even in a condition to remonstrate with dignity? The just imputations on our own faith, in respect to the same treaty, ought first to be removed. Are we entitled, by nature and compact, to a free participation in the navigation of the Mississippi? Spain excludes us from it. Is public credit an indispensable resource in time of public danger? We seem to have abandoned its cause as desperate and irretrievable. Is commerce of importance to national wealth? Ours is at the lowest point of declension. Is respectability in the eyes of foreign powers a safeguard against foreign encroachments? The imbecility of our government even forbids them to treat with us: our ambassadors abroad are the mere pageants of mimic sovereignty.

Is a violent and unnatural decrease in the value of land a symptom of national distress? The price of improved land, in most parts of the country, is much lower than can be accounted for by the quantity of waste land at market, and can only be fully explained by that want of private and public confidence which are so alarmingly prevalent among all ranks, and which have a direct tendency to depreciate property of every kind. Is private credit the friend and patron of industry? That most useful kind which relates to borrowing and lending is reduced within the narrowest limits, and this still more from an opinion of insecurity than from a scarcity of money. To shorten an enumeration of particulars which can afford neither pleasure nor instruction, it may in general be demanded what indication is there of national disorder, poverty, and insignificance that could befall a community so peculiarly blest with natural advantages as we are, which does not form a part of the dark catalog of our public misfortunes?

This is the melancholy situation to which we have been brought by those very maxims and counsels which would now deter us from adopting the proposed constitution; and which, not content with having conducted us to the brink of a precipice, seem resolved to plunge us into the abyss that awaits us below. Here, my countrymen, impelled by every motive that ought to influence an enlightened people, let us make a firm stand for our safety, our tranquillity, our dignity, our reputation. Let us at last break the fatal charm which has too long seduced us from the paths of felicity and prosperity.

It is true, as has been before observed, that facts too stubborn to be resisted have produced a species of general assent to the abstract proposition that there exist material defects in our national system; but the usefulness of the concession, on the part of the old adversaries of federal measures, is destroyed by a strenuous opposition to a remedy, upon the only principles that can give it a chance of success. While they admit that the government of the United States is destitute of energy, they contend against conferring upon it those powers which are requisite to supply that energy. They seem still to aim at things repugnant and irreconcilable; at an augmentation of federal authority, without a diminution of State authority; at sovereignty in the Union, and complete independence in the members. They still, in fine, seem to cherish with blind devotion the political monster of an *imperium in imperio*. This renders a full display of the principal defects of the confederation necessary in order to show that the evils we experience do not proceed from minute or partial imperfections, but from fundamental errors in the structure of the building, which can not be amended otherwise than by an alteration in the very elements and main pillars of the fabric.

The great and radical vice in the construction of the existing confederation is in the principle of legislation for states or governments in their corporate or collective capacities, and as contradistinguished from the individuals of whom they consist. Tho this principle does not run through all the powers delegated to the Union; yet it pervades and governs those on which the efficacy of the rest depends: except as to the rule of apportionment, the United States have an indefinite discretion to make requisitions for men and money; but they have no authority to raise either by regulations extending to the individual citizens of America. The consequence of this is that, tho in theory their resolutions concerning those objects are laws constitutionally binding on the members of the Union, yet in practise they are mere recommendations, which the States observe or disregard at their option.

It is a singular instance of the capriciousness of the human mind that after all the admonitions we have had from experience on this head, there should still be found men who object to the new constitution for deviating from a principle which has been found the bane of the old; and which is, in itself, evidently incompatible with the idea of a government; a principle, in short, which, if it is to be executed at all, must substitute the violent and sanguinary agency of the sword to the mild influence of the magistracy.

ALEXANDER HAMILTON

II

HIS REASONS FOR NOT DECLINING BURR'S CHALLENGE [2]

On my expected interview with Col. Burr, I think it proper to make some remarks explanatory of my conduct, motives, and views. I was certainly desirous of avoiding this interview for the most urgent reasons:

1. My religious and moral principles are strongly opposed to the practise of duelling, and it would ever give me pain to be obliged to shed the blood of a fellow creature in a private combat forbidden by the law.

2. My wife and children are extremely dear to me, and my life is of the utmost importance to them in various views.

3. I feel a sense of obligation toward my creditors, who, in case of accident to me, by the forced sale of my property, may be in some degree sufferers. I did not think myself at liberty, as a man of probity, lightly to expose them to this hazard.

4. I am conscious of no ill-will toward Col. Burr, distinct from political opposition, which, as I trust, has proceeded from pure and upright motives.

Lastly, I shall hazard much and can probably gain nothing by the issue of this interview.

---

[2] Written the day before the duel, which took place in Weehawken, N. J., on July 11, 1804. Hamilton, wounded, was taken to his house in the upper part of Manhattan Island and there died on the following day. This statement is now printed in Volume VIII of the "Works of Hamilton."

But it was, as I conceive, impossible to avoid it. There were intrinsic difficulties in the thing, an artificial embarrassment from the manner of proceeding on the part of Col. Burr.

Intrinsic, because it is not to be denied that my animadversion on the political principles, character and views of Col. Burr have been extremely severe; and on different occasions I, in common with many others, have made very unfavorable criticisms on particular instances of the private conduct of this gentleman. In proportion as these impressions were entertained with sincerity and uttered with motives and for purposes which might appear to me commendable would be the difficulty (until they could be removed by evidence of their being erroneous) of explanation or apology. The disavowal required of me by Col. Burr in a general and indefinite form was out of my power, if it had really been proper for me to submit to be questioned, but I was sincerely of the opinion that this could not be, and in this opinion I was confirmed by a very moderate and judicious friend whom I consulted. Besides that, Col. Burr appeared to me to assume, in the first instance, a tone unnecessarily peremptory and menacing, and, in the second, positively offensive. Yet I wished as far as might be practicable to leave a door open to accommodation. This, I think, will be inferred from the written communication made by me and by my directions, and would be confirmed by the conversation between Mr. Van Ness and myself which arose out of the subject. I am not sure whether, under all the circumstances, I did not go further in the attempt to accommodate than a punctilious delicacy will justify. If so, I hope the motives I have stated will excuse me. It is not my design by what I have said to affix any odium on the conduct of Col. Burr in this case. He doubtless has heard of animadversions of mine which bore very hard upon him, and it is probable that, as usual, they were accompanied with some falsehoods. He may have supposed himself under the necessity of acting as he has done. I hope the ground of his proceeding is such as ought to satisfy his own conscience. I trust, at the same time, that the world will do me the justice to believe that I have not censured him on light grounds nor from unworthy motives. I certainly have had strong reasons for what I have said, tho it is possible in some particulars I may have been influenced by misconstructions or misinformation. It is also my ardent wish that I may have been more mistaken than I think I have been, and that he, by his future conduct, may show himself worthy of all confidence and esteem and prove an ornament and a blessing to the country as well, because it is possible I may have injured Col. Burr, however convinced myself that my opinions and declarations may have been well founded.

As for my general principles and temper in relation to similar affairs, I have resolved, if our interview is conducted in the usual manner, and it pleases God to give me the opportunity, to reserve and throw away my first fire, and I have thoughts even of reserving my second fire, and thus giving a double opportunity to Col. Burr to pause and reflect. It is not, however, my intention to enter into any explanation on the ground. Apology, from principle, I hope, rather than pride, is out of the question. To those who, with me abhorring the practise of duelling, may think that I ought on no account to have added to the number of examples, I answer that my relative situation as well in public as in private, enforcing all the considerations which constitute what men of the world denominate honor, inspired in me (as I thought) a peculiar necessity not to decline the call. The ability to be useful in future, whether in resisting mischief or in effecting good, in those crises of our public affairs which seem lately to happen would probably be inseparable from a conformity with public prejudice in this particular.[3]

[3] Among the Hamilton papers is a letter addrest as follows to Mrs. Hamilton, dated the day before the duel:

"This letter, my dear Eliza, will not be delivered to you unless I shall first have terminated my earthly career, to begin, as I humbly hope from redeeming grace and divine mercy, a happy immortality. If it had been possible for me to have avoided the interview, my love for you and my precious children would have been alone a decisive motive. But it was not possible without sacrifice which would have rendered me unworthy of your esteem. I need not tell you of the pangs I feel from the idea of quitting you and exposing you to the anguish I know you would feel. Nor could I dwell on the topic lest it should unman me. The consolations of religion, my beloved, can alone support you; and these you have a right to enjoy. Fly to the bosom of your God and be comforted. With my last idea I shall cherish the sweet hope of meeting you in a better world. Adieu, best of wives, best of women. Embrace all my darling children for me."

JOHN QUINCY ADAMS

Born in Massachusetts in 1767, died in Washington in 1848; son of John Adams; graduated from Harvard in 1787; admitted to the bar in 1791; minister to the Netherlands in 1794-97; minister to Prussia in 1797-1801; Senator from Massachusetts in 1803-08; professor at Harvard in 1806-09; minister to Russia in 1809-14; minister to England in 1815-17; Secretary of State in 1817-25; elected President in 1824; defeated for the Presidency by Jackson in 1828; Member of Congress in 1831-48; unsuccessful candidate for Governor of Massachusetts in 1834; his "Diary" published in 1874-77.

I

OF HIS MOTHER[1]

THERE is not a virtue that can abide in the female heart but it was the ornament of hers. She had been fifty-four years the delight of my father's heart, the sweetener of all his toils, the comforter of all his sorrows, the sharer and heightener of all his joys. It was but the last time when I saw my father that he told me, with an ejaculation of gratitude to the Giver of every good and every perfect gift, that in all the vicissitudes of his fortunes, through all the good report and evil report of the world, in all his

[1] From the "Diary." Adams's mother was Abigail Smith Adams, daughter of the Rev. William Smith of Weymouth, Mass. Her letters, which have been much admired, have been published in a work entitled "The Familiar Letters of John Adams and his Wife."

struggles and in all his sorrows, the affectionate participation and cheering encouragement of his wife had been his never-failing support, without which he was sure he should never have lived through them. . . .

Never have I known another human being the perpetual object of whose life was so unremittingly to do good. It was a necessity of her nature. Yet so unostentatious, so unconscious even of her own excellence that even the objects of her kindness often knew not whence it came. She had seen the world—its glories without being dazzled; its vices and follies without being infected by them. She had suffered often and severely from fits of long and painful sickness, always with calmness and resignation. She had a profound, but not an obtrusive sensibility. She was always cheerful, never frivolous; she had neither gall nor guile.

Her attention to the domestic economy of her family was unrivaled—rising with the dawn, and superintending the household concerns with indefatigable and all-foreseeing care. She had a warm and lively relish for literature, for social conversation, for whatever was interesting in the occurrences of the time, and even in political affairs. She had been, during the war of our Revolution, an ardent patriot, and the earliest lesson of unbounded devotion to the cause of their country that her children received was from her. She had the most delicate sense of propriety of conduct, but nothing uncharitable, nothing bitter. Her price was indeed above rubies.

II

THE MORAL TAINT INHERENT IN SLAVERY [3]

AFTER this meeting I walked home with Calhoun, who said that the principles which I had avowed were just and noble; but that in the Southern country, whenever they were mentioned, they were always understood as applying only to white men. Domestic labor was confined to the blacks, and such was the prejudice that if he, who was the most popular man in his district, were to keep a white servant in his house, his character and reputation would be irretrievably ruined.

I said that this confounding of the ideas of servitude and labor was one of the bad effects of slavery; but he thought it attended with many excellent consequences. It did not apply to all kinds of labor—not, for example, to farming. He himself had often held the plow; so had his father. Manufacturing and mechanical labor was not degrading. It was only manual labor—the proper work of slaves. No white person could descend to that. And it was the best guarantee to equality among the whites. It produced an unvarying level among them. It not only did not excite, but did not even admit of inequalities by which one white man could domineer over another.

I told Calhoun I could not see things in the

[3] From the "Diary."

same light. It is, in truth, all perverted sentiment—mistaking labor for slavery, and dominion for freedom. The discussion of the Missouri question has betrayed the secret of their souls. In the abstract they admit that slavery is an evil, they disclaim all participation in the introduction of it, and cast it all upon the shoulders of our old granddam Britain. But when probed to the quick upon it, they show at the bottom of their souls pride and vainglory in their condition of masterdom. They fancy themselves more generous and noble-hearted than the plain freemen who labor for subsistence. They look down upon the simplicity of a Yankee's manners, because he has no habits of overbearing like theirs and can not treat negroes like dogs.

It is among the evils of slavery that it taints the very sources of moral principle. It establishes false estimates of virtue and vice; for what can be more false and heartless than this doctrine which makes the first and holiest rights of humanity to depend upon the color of the skin? It perverts human reason, and reduces man endowed with logical powers to maintain that slavery is sanctioned by the Christian religion, that slaves are happy and contented in their condition, that between master and slave there are ties of mutual attachment and affection, that the virtues of the master are refined and exalted by the degradation of the slave; while at the same time they vent execrations upon the slave-trade, curse Britain for having given them slaves, burn at the stake negroes convicted of crimes for the terror of the example, and writhe in agonies of fear at the very mention of human rights as applicable to men of color. The impression produced upon my mind by the progress of this discussion is that the bargain between freedom and slavery contained in the Constitution of the United States is morally and politically vicious, inconsistent with the principles upon which alone our Revolution can be justified; cruel and oppressive, by riveting the chains of slavery, by pledging the faith of freedom to maintain and perpetuate the tyranny of the master; and grossly unequal and impolitic, by admitting that slaves are at once enemies to be kept in subjection, property to be secured or restored to their owners, and persons not to be represented themselves, but for whom their masters are privileged with nearly a double share of representation.

The consequence has been that this slave representation has governed the Union. Benjamin portioned above his brethren has ravened as a wolf. In the morning he has devoured the prey, and at night he has divided the spoil. It would be no difficult matter to prove, by reviewing the history of the Union under this Constitution, that almost everything which has contributed to the honor and welfare of the nation has been accomplished in despite of them or forced upon them, and that everything unpropitious and dishonorable, including the blunders and follies of their adversaries, may be traced to them. I have favored this Missouri compromise, believing it to be all that could be effected under the present Constitution, and from extreme unwillingness to put the Union at hazard. But perhaps it would have been a wiser as well as a bolder course to have persisted in the restriction upon Missouri, till it should have terminated in a convention of the States to amend and revise the Constitution. This would have produced a new Union of thirteen or fourteen States unpolluted with slavery, with a great and glorious object to effect, namely, that of rallying to their standard the other States by the universal emancipation of their slaves. If the Union must be dissolved, slavery is precisely the question upon which it ought to break. For the present, however, this contest is laid asleep.

WILLIAM E. CHANNING

Born in Rhode Island in 1780, died in Vermont in 1842; clergyman, author and philanthropist; one of the chief founders of Unitarianism; pastor of the Federal Street Church in Boston in 1803; his complete works published in 1848.

OF GREATNESS IN NAPOLEON [1]

WE close our view of Bonaparte's character by saying that his original propensities, released from restraint, and pampered by indulgence to a degree seldom allowed to mortals, grew up into a spirit of despotism as stern and absolute as ever usurped the human heart. The love of power and supremacy absorbed, consumed him. No other passion, no domestic attachment, no private friendship, no love of pleasure, no relish for letters or the arts, no human sympathy, no human weakness, divided his mind with the passion for dominion and for dazzling manifestations of his power. Before this, duty, honor, love, humanity fell prostrate. Josephine, we are told, was dear to him; but the devoted wife, who had stood firm and faithful in the day of his doubtful fortunes, was cast off in his prosperity to make room for a stranger, who might be more sub-

[1] From a review of Sir Walter Scott's "Life of Napoleon," printed in the *Christian Examiner* in 1827 and now included in Volume I of the collected edition of Channing's writings.

servient to his power. He was affectionate, we are told, to his brothers and mother; but his brothers, the moment they ceased to be his tools, were disgraced; and his mother, it is said, was not allowed to sit in the presence of her imperial son. He was sometimes softened, we are told, by the sight of the field of battle strewn with the wounded and dead. But, if the Moloch of his ambition claimed new heaps of slain tomorrow, it was never denied. With all his sensibility, he gave millions to the sword with as little compunction as he would have brushed away so many insects which had infested his march. To him all human will, desire, power were to bend. His superiority none might question. He insulted the fallen, who had contracted the guilt of opposing his progress; and not even woman's loveliness, and the dignity of a queen could give shelter from his contumely. His allies were his vassals, nor was their vassalage concealed. Too lofty to use the arts of conciliation, preferring command to persuasion, overbearing, and all-grasping, he spread distrust, exasperation, fear, and revenge through Europe; and, when the day of retribution came, the old antipathies and mutual jealousies of nations were swallowed up in one burning purpose to prostrate the common tyrant, the universal foe.

Such was Napoleon Bonaparte. But some will say he was still a great man. This we mean not to deny. But we would have it understood that there are various kinds or orders of greatness, and that the highest did not belong to Bonaparte. There are different orders of greatness. Among these the first rank is unquestionably due to moral greatness, or magnanimity; to that sublime energy by which the soul, smitten with the love of virtue, binds itself indissolubly, for life and for death, to truth and duty; espouses as its own the interests of human nature; scorns all meanness and defies all peril; hears in its own conscience a voice louder than threatenings and thunders; withstands all the powers of the universe which would sever it from the cause of freedom and religion; reposes an unfaltering trust in God in the darkest hour, and is ever "ready to be offered up" on the altar of its country or of mankind.

Of this moral greatness, which throws all other forms of greatness into obscurity, we see not a trace in Napoleon. Tho clothed with the power of a god, the thought of consecrating himself to the introduction of a new and higher era, to the exaltation of the character and condition of his race, seems never to have dawned on his mind. The spirit of disinterestedness and self-sacrifice seems not to have waged a moment's war with self-will and ambition. His ruling passions, indeed, were singularly at variance with magnanimity. Moral greatness has too much simplicity, is too unostentatious, too self-subsistent and enters into others' interests with too much heartiness, to live an hour for what Napoleon always lived, to make itself the theme, and gaze, and wonder of a dazzled world. Next to moral, comes intellectual greatness, or genius in the highest sense of that word; and by this we mean that sublime capacity of thought, through which the soul, smitten with the love of the true and the beautiful, essays to comprehend the universe, soars into the heavens, penetrates the earth, penetrates itself, questions the past, anticipates the future, traces out the general and all-comprehending laws of nature, binds together by innumerable affinities and relations all the objects of its knowledge, rises from the finite and transient to the infinite and the everlasting, frames to itself from its own fulness lovelier and sublimer forms than it beholds, discerns the harmonies between the world within and the world without us, and finds in every region of the universe types and interpreters of its own deep mysteries and glorious inspirations. This is the greatness which belongs to philosophers, and to the master-spirits in poetry and the fine arts.

Next comes the greatness of action; and by this we mean the sublime power of conceiving bold and extensive plans; of constructing and bringing to bear on a mighty object a complicated machinery of means, energies, and arrangements, and of accomplishing great outward effects. To this head belongs the greatness of Bonaparte, and that he possest it we need not prove, and none will be hardy enough to deny. A man who raised himself from obscurity to a throne, who changed the face of the world, who made himself felt through powerful and civilized nations, who sent the terror of his name across seas and oceans, whose will was pronounced and feared as destiny, whose donatives were crowns, whose antechamber was thronged by submissive princes, who broke down the awful barrier of the Alps and made them a highway, and whose fame was spread beyond the boundaries of civilization to the steppes of the Cossack, and the deserts of the

Arab; a man who has left this record of himself in history, has taken out of our hands the question whether he shall be called great. All must concede to him a sublime power of action, an energy equal to great effects.

JOHN JAMES AUDUBON

Born in New Orleans in 1780, died in New York in 1857; educated in France, where he was a pupil of David; failing to establish himself in business in America, he devoted his time to the study of birds, making long excursions on foot; published his "Birds of America" in 1827-30, the price per copy being $1,000; published his "Ornithological Biography" in 5 volumes in 1831-39.

WHERE THE MOCKING-BIRD DWELLS[1]

It is where the great magnolia shoots up its majestic trunk, crowned with evergreen leaves, and decorated with a thousand beautiful flowers, that perfume the air around; where the forests and fields are adorned with blossoms of every hue; where the golden orange ornaments the gardens and groves; where bignonias of various kinds interlace their climbing stems around the white-flowered stuartia, and, mounting still higher, cover the summits of the lofty trees around, accompanied with innumerable vines that here and there festoon the dense foliage of the magnificent woods, lending to the vernal breeze a slight portion of the perfume of their clustered flowers; where a genial warmth seldom forsakes the atmosphere; where berries and fruits of all descriptions are met with at every step—in a word, it is where Nature seems to have paused,

[1] From Volume II, page 187, of the "Birds of America," edition of 1841.

JOHN JAMES AUDUBON

as she passed over the earth, and, opening her stores, to have strewed with unsparing hand the diversified seeds from which have sprung all the beautiful and splendid forms which I should in vain attempt to describe, that the mocking-bird should have fixt its abode—there only that its wondrous song should be heard.

But where is that favored land? It is in that great continent to whose distant shores Europe has sent forth her adventurous sons, to wrest for themselves a habitation from the wild inhabitants of the forest, and to convert the neglected soil into fields of exuberant fertility. It is, reader, in Louisiana that these bounties of nature are in the greatest perfection. It is there that you should listen to the love song of the mocking-bird, as I at this moment do. See how he flies round his mate, with motions as light as those of the butterfly! His tail is widely expanded, he mounts in the air to a small distance, describes a circle, and, again alighting, approaches his beloved one, his eyes gleaming with delight, for she has already promised to be his and his only. His beautiful wings are gently raised, he bows to his love, and, again bouncing upward, opens his bill and pours forth his melody, full of exultation at the conquest he has made.

They are not the soft sounds of the flute or the hautboy that I hear, but the sweeter notes of nature's own music. The mellowness of the song, the varied modulations and gradations, the extent of its compass, the great brilliancy of execution are unrivaled. There is probably no bird in the world that possesses all the musical qualifications of this king of song, who has derived all from Nature's self. Yes, reader, all!

No sooner has he again alighted, and the conjugal contract has been sealed, than, as if his breast were about to be rent with delight, he again pours forth his notes with more softness and richness than before. He now soars higher, glancing around with a vigilant eye, to assure himself that none has witnessed his bliss. When these love scenes are over, he dances through the air, full of animation and delight, and, as if to convince his lovely mate that to enrich her hopes he has much more love in store, he that moment begins anew, and imitates all the notes which nature has imparted to the other songsters of the grove.

WASHINGTON IRVING

Born in New York in 1783, died at Sunnyside in 1859; studied law, but owing to ill health went abroad in 1804, remaining two years; returning home, began to publish "Salmagundi" in company with James K. Paulding; published in 1809 his "History of New York," which established his literary reputation; went abroad in 1815, remaining until 1832; attached to the legation in Madrid in 1826; secretary of legation in London in 1829; minister to Spain in 1842; published the "Sketch Book" in 1819-20, "Bracebridge Hall" in 1822, "Tales of a Traveler" in 1824, "Christopher Columbus" in 1828, "Conquest of Granada" in 1829, "The Alhambra" in 1832, "Life of Washington" in 1855-59; author of many other books; his "Life and Letters" published in 1861-67.

I

THE LAST OF THE DUTCH GOVERNORS OF NEW YORK[1]

PETER STUYVESANT was the last, and, like the renowned Wouter Van Twiller, the best of our ancient Dutch governors. Wouter having surpassed all who preceded him, and Peter, or Piet, as he was sociably called by the old Dutch burghers, who were ever prone to familiarize names, having never been equaled by any successor. He was, in fact, the very man fitted by nature to retrieve the desperate fortunes of her beloved province, had not the Fates, those most potent

[1] From Book V, Chapter I, of "Knickerbocker's History of New York."

and unrelenting of all ancient spinsters, destined them to inextricable confusion.

To say merely that he was a hero would be doing him great injustice—he was in truth a combination of heroes—for he was of a sturdy, raw-boned make like Ajax Telamon, with a pair of round shoulders that Hercules would have given his hide for (meaning his lion's hide) when he undertook to ease old Atlas of his load. He was, moreover, as Plutarch describes Coriolanus, not only terrible for the force of his arm, but likewise of his voice, which sounded as tho it came out of a barrel; and, like the self-same warrior, he possest a sovereign contempt for the sovereign people, and an iron aspect, which was enough of itself to make the very bowels of his adversaries quake with terror and dismay. All this martial excellency of appearance was inexpressibly heightened by an accidental advantage, with which I am surprised that neither Homer nor Virgil have graced any of their heroes. This was nothing less than a wooden leg,[2] which was the only prize he had gained in bravely fighting the battles of his country, but of which he was so proud that he was often heard to declare he valued it more than all his other limbs put together; indeed, so highly did he

---

[2] Stuyvesant lost his leg in the West Indies, where he was serving in a Dutch command. In 1634 he became director of the colony of Curaçao. In 1636 he was made director-general of the Dutch colony in North America. He retained this office, in which he was notably efficient, until the surrender of New Amsterdam to the English in 1664. Stuyvesant spent the remainder of his life in New York on a farm called the Bowery, where he died in 1672. He was buried in grounds where now stands St. Mark's Church.

esteem it that he had it gallantly enchased and relieved with silver devices, which caused it to be related in divers histories and legends that he wore a silver leg.

Like that choleric warrior Achilles, he was somewhat subject to extempore bursts of passion, which were rather unpleasant to his favorites and attendants, whose perceptions he was apt to quicken, after the manner of his illustrious imitator, Peter the Great, by anointing their shoulders with his walking-staff.

Tho I can not find that he had read Plato, or Aristotle, or Hobbes, or Bacon, or Algernon Sydney, or Tom Paine, yet did he sometimes manifest a shrewdness and sagacity in his measures that one would hardly expect from a man who did not know Greek, and had never studied the ancients. True it is, and I confess it with sorrow, that he had an unreasonable aversion to experiments, and was fond of governing his province after the simplest manner; but then he contrived to keep it in better order than did the erudite Kieft,[3] tho he had all the philosophers, ancient and modern, to assist and perplex him. I must likewise own that he made but very few laws; but then again he took care that those few were rigidly and impartially enforced: and I do not know but justice on the whole was

---

[3] William Kieft, the predecessor of Stuyvesant in the government of New Amsterdam, was a tyrannical, blundering administrator, whose rule was marked by disastrous wars with the Indians and dissension among his own people which nearly ruined the province. He was recalled by the home government, and while on his way to Holland was lost in the wreck, on the English coast, of the ship in which he had sailed.

as well administered as if there had been volumes of sage acts and statutes yearly made, and daily neglected and forgotten.

He was, in fact, the very reverse of his predecessors, being neither tranquil and inert, like Walter the Doubter, nor restless and fidgeting, like William the Testy; but a man, or rather a governor of such uncommon activity and decision of mind that he never sought nor accepted the advice of others; depending bravely upon his single head, as would a hero of yore upon his single arm, to carry him through all difficulties and dangers. To tell the simple truth, he wanted nothing more to complete him as a statesman than to think always right; for no one can say but that he always acted as he thought. He was never a man to flinch when he found himself in a scrape; but to dash forward through thick and thin, trusting, by hook or by crook, to make all things straight in the end. In a word, he possest, in an eminent degree, that great quality in a statesman, called perseverance by the polite, but nicknamed obstinacy by the vulgar. A wonderful salve for official blunders; since he who perseveres in error without flinching gets the credit of boldness and consistency, while he who wavers in seeking to do what is right gets stigmatized as a trimmer. This much is certain; and it is a maxim well worthy the attention of all legislators, great and small, who stand shaking in the wind, irresolute which way to steer, that a ruler who follows his own will pleases himself; while he who seeks to satisfy the wishes and whims of others runs great risk of pleasing nobody. There is nothing, too, like putting down one's foot resolutely, when in doubt, and letting things take their course. The clock that stands still points right twice in the four-and-twenty hours: while others may keep going continually and be continually going wrong.

Nor did this magnanimous quality escape the discernment of the good people of Nieuw Nederlandts; on the contrary, so much were they struck with the independent will and vigorous resolution displayed on all occasions by their new governor, that they universally called him Hard-Koppig Piet; or Peter the Headstrong—a great compliment to the strength of his understanding.

If, from all that I have said, thou dost not gather, worthy reader, that Peter Stuyvesant was a tough, sturdy, valiant, weather-beaten, mettlesome, obstinate, leather-sided, lion-hearted, generous-spirited old governor, either I have written to but little purpose, or thou art very dull at drawing conclusions.

II

THE AWAKENING OF RIP VAN WINKLE[4]

On waking, he found himself on the green knoll whence he had first seen the old man of the glen. He rubbed his eyes—it was a bright sunny morning. The birds were hopping and

[4] From the "Sketch Book," originally published in parts in 1819-20, "Rip Van Winkle" being included in the first number. Irving's story has furnished the material for eight or ten plays, the most successful of which was written by Dion Boucicault. Boucicault's work was materially altered by Joseph Jefferson into the play now closely associated with Jefferson's fame.

twittering among the bushes, and the eagle was wheeling aloft, and breasting the pure mountain breeze. "Surely," thought Rip, "I have not slept here all night." He recalled the occurrences before he fell asleep. The strange man with a keg of liquor—the mountain ravine—the wild retreat among the rocks—the wo-begone party at nine-pins—the flagon—"Oh! that flagon! that wicked flagon!" thought Rip—"what excuse shall I make to Dame Van Winkle!"

He looked round for his gun, but in place of the clean well-oiled fowling-piece, he found an old firelock lying by him, the barrel incrusted with rust, the lock falling off, and the stock worm-eaten. He now suspected that the grave roysterers of the mountain had put a trick upon him, and, having dosed him with liquor, had robbed him of his gun. Wolf, too, had disappeared, but he might have strayed away after a squirrel or partridge. He whistled after him and shouted his name, but all in vain; the echoes repeated his whistle and shout, but no dog was to be seen.

He determined to revisit the scene of the last evening's gambol, and if he met with any of the party, to demand his dog and gun. As he rose to walk, he found himself stiff in the joints, and wanting in his usual activity. "These mountain beds do not agree with me," thought Rip, "and if this frolic should lay me up with a fit of the rheumatism, I shall have a blest time with Dame Van Winkle." With some difficulty he got down into the glen: he found the gully up which he and his companion had ascended the preceding evening; but to his astonishment a mountain stream was now foaming down it, leaping from rock to rock, and filling the glen with babbling murmurs. He, however, made shift to scramble up its sides, working his toilsome way through thickets of birch, sassafras, and witch-hazel, and sometimes tript up or entangled by the wild grape-vines that twisted their coils or tendrils from tree to tree, and spread a kind of network in his path.

At length he reached to where the ravine had opened through the cliffs to the amphitheater; but no traces of such opening remained. The rocks presented a high impenetrable wall over which the torrent came tumbling in a sheet of feathery foam, and fell into a broad deep basin, black from the shadows of the surrounding forest. Here, then, poor Rip was brought to a stand. He again called and whistled after his dog; he was only answered by the cawing of a flock of idle crows, sporting high in air about a dry tree that overhung a sunny precipice; and who, secure in their elevation, seemed to look down and scoff at the poor man's perplexities. What was to be done? the morning was passing away, and Rip felt famished for want of his breakfast. He grieved to give up his dog and gun; he dreaded to meet his wife; but it would not do to starve among the mountains. He shook his head, shouldered the rusty firelock, and, with a heart full of trouble and anxiety, turned his steps homeward.

As he approached the village he met a number of people, but none whom he knew, which somewhat surprized him, for he had thought himself acquainted with every one in the country round.

Their dress, too, was of a different fashion from that to which he was accustomed. They all stared at him with equal marks of surprize, and whenever they cast their eyes upon him, invariably stroked their chins. The constant recurrence of this gesture induced Rip, involuntarily, to do the same, when, to his astonishment, he found his beard had grown a foot long!

He had now entered the skirts of the village. A troop of strange children ran at his heels, hooting after him, and pointing at his gray beard. The dogs, too, not one of which he recognized for an old acquaintance, barked at him as he passed. The very village was altered; it was larger and more populous. There were rows of houses which he had never seen before, and those which had been his familiar haunts had disappeared. Strange names were over the doors—strange faces at the windows—everything was strange. His mind now misgave him; he began to doubt whether both he and the world around him were not bewitched. Surely this was his native village, which he had left but the day before. There stood the Catskill Mountains—there ran the silver Hudson at a distance—there was every hill and dale precisely as it had always been—Rip was sorely perplexed—"That flagon last night," thought he, "has addled my poor head sadly!"

It was with some difficulty that he found the way to his own house, which he approached with silent awe, expecting every moment to hear the shrill voice of Dame Van Winkle. He found the house gone to decay—the roof fallen in, the windows shattered, and the doors off the hinges. A half-starved dog that looked like Wolf was skulking about it. Rip called him by name, but the cur snarled, showed his teeth, and passed on. This was an unkind cut indeed—"My very dog," sighed poor Rip, "has forgotten me!"

He entered the house, which, to tell the truth, Dame Van Winkle had always kept in neat order. It was empty, forlorn, and apparently abandoned. This desolateness overcame all his connubial fears—he called loudly for his wife and children—the lonely chambers rang for a moment with his voice, and then all again was silence.

He now hurried forth, and hastened to his old resort, the village inn—but it too was gone. A large rickety wooden building stood in its place, with great gaping windows, some of them broken and mended with old hats and petticoats, and over the door was painted, "The Union Hotel, by Jonathan Doolittle." Instead of the great tree that used to shelter the quiet little Dutch inn of yore, there now was reared a tall naked pole, with something on the top that looked like a red night-cap, and from it was fluttering a flag, on which was a singular assemblage of stars and stripes—all this was strange and incomprehensible. He recognized on the sign, however, the ruby face of King George, under which he had smoked so many a peaceful pipe; but even this was singularly metamorphosed. The red coat was changed for one of blue and buff, a sword was held in the hand instead of a scepter, the head was decorated with a cocked hat, and underneath was painted in large characters, GENERAL WASHINGTON.

There was, as usual, a crowd of folk about the

door, but none that Rip recollected. The very character of the people seemed changed. There was a busy, bustling, disputatious tone about it, instead of the accustomed phlegm and drowsy tranquillity. He looked in vain for the sage Nicholas Vedder, with his broad face, double chin, and fair long pipe, uttering clouds of tobacco-smoke instead of idle speeches; or Van Bummel, the schoolmaster, doling forth the contents of an ancient newspaper. In place of these, a lean, bilious-looking fellow, with his pockets full of handbills, was haranguing vehemently about rights of citizens—elections—members of Congress—liberty—Bunker Hill—heroes of seventy-six—and other words, which were a perfect Babylonish jargon to the bewildered Van Winkle.

The appearance of Rip, with his long grizzled beard, his rusty fowling-piece, his uncouth dress, and an army of women and children at his heels, soon attracted the attention of the tavern politicians. They crowded round him, eyeing him from head to foot with great curiosity. The orator bustled up to him, and, drawing him partly aside, inquired "on which side he voted?" Rip stared in vacant stupidity. Another short but busy little fellow pulled him by the arm, and, rising on tiptoe, inquired in his ear "whether he was Federal or Democrat?" Rip was equally at a loss to comprehend the question; when a knowing, self-important old gentleman, in a sharp cocked hat, made his way through the crowd, putting them to right and left with his elbows as he passed, and planting himself before Van Winkle, with arms akimbo, the other resting on his cane, his keen eyes and sharp hat penetrating, as it were, into his very soul, demanded in an austere tone "what brought him to the election with a gun on his shoulder, and a mob at his heels, and whether he meant to breed a riot in the village?" "Alas! gentlemen," cried Rip, somewhat dismayed, "I am a poor quiet man, a native of the place, and a loyal subject of the King, God bless him!"

Here a general shout burst from the bystanders—"A Tory! a Tory! a spy! a refugee! hustle him! away with him!" It was with great difficulty that the self-important man in the cocked hat restored order; and, having assumed a tenfold austerity of brow, demanded again of the unknown culprit what he came there for, and whom he was seeking? The poor man humbly assured him that he meant no harm, but merely came there in search of some of his neighbors, who used to keep about the tavern.

"Well—who are they?—name them."

Rip bethought himself a moment, and inquired, "Where's Nicholas Vedder?"

There was a silence for a little while, when an old man replied, in a thin piping voice, "Nicholas Vedder! why, he is dead and gone these eighteen years! There was a wooden tombstone in the churchyard that used to tell all about him, but that's rotten and gone too."

"Where's Brom Dutcher?"

"Oh, he went off to the army in the beginning of the war; some say he was killed at the storming of Stony Point—others say he was drowned in a squall at the foot of Antony's Nose. I don't know—he never came back again."

"Where's Van Bummel, the schoolmaster?"

"He went off to the wars too, was a great militia general, and is now in Congress."

Rip's heart died away at hearing of these sad changes in his home and friends, and finding himself thus alone in the world. Every answer puzzled him too, by treating of such enormous lapses of time, and of matters which he could not understand: war—Congress—Stony Point; he had no courage to ask after any more friends, but cried out in despair, "Does nobody here know Rip Van Winkle?"

"Oh, Rip Van Winkle!" exclaimed two or three—"oh, to be sure! that's Rip Van Winkle yonder, leaning against the tree."

Rip looked, and beheld a precise counterpart of himself, as he went up the mountain: apparently as lazy, and certainly as ragged. The poor fellow was now completely confounded. He doubted his own identity, and whether he was himself or another man. In the midst of his bewilderment, the man in the cocked hat demanded who he was, and what was his name?

"God knows," exclaimed he, at his wit's end; "I'm not myself—I'm somebody else—that's me yonder—no—that's somebody else got into my shoes—I was myself last night, but I fell asleep on the mountain, and they've changed my gun, and everything's changed, and I'm changed, and I can't tell what's my name, or who I am!"

The bystanders began now to look at each other, nod, wink significantly, and tap their fingers against their foreheads. There was a whisper, also, about securing the gun, and keeping the old fellow from doing mischief, at the very suggestion of which the self-important man in the cocked hat retired with some precipitation. At this critical moment a fresh comely woman prest through the throng to get a peep at the gray-bearded man. She had a chubby child in her arms, which, frightened at his looks, began to cry. "Hush, Rip," cried she, "hush, you little fool; the old man won't hurt you." The name of the child, the air of the mother, the tone of her voice, all awakened a train of recollections in his mind. "What is your name, my good woman," asked he.

"Judith Gardenier."

"And your father's name?"

"Ah, poor man, Rip Van Winkle was his name, but it's twenty years since he went away from home with his gun, and never has been heard of since—his dog came home without him; but whether he shot himself, or was carried away by the Indians, nobody can tell. I was then but a little girl."

Rip had but one question more to ask; but he put it with a faltering voice:

"Where's your mother?"

"Oh, she too had died but a short time since; she broke a blood-vessel in a fit of passion at a New England peddler."

There was a drop of comfort, at least, in this intelligence. The honest man could contain himself no longer. He caught his daughter and her child in his arms. "I am your father!" cried he—"Young Rip Van Winkle once—old Rip Van Winkle now!—Does nobody know poor Rip Van Winkle?"

All stood amazed, until an old woman, tottering out from among the crowd, put her hand to her brow, and peering under it in his face for a moment, exclaimed, "Sure enough! it is Rip Van Winkle—it is himself! Welcome home again, old neighbor—why, where have you been these twenty long years?"

Rip's story was soon told, for the whole twenty years had been to him but as one night. The neighbors stared when they heard it; some were seen to wink at each other, and put their tongues in their cheeks: and the self-important man in the cocked hat, who, when the alarm was over, had returned to the field, screwed down the corners of his mouth, and shook his head—upon which there was a general shaking of the head throughout the assemblage.

It was determined, however, to take the opinion of old Peter Vanderdonk, who was seen slowly advancing up the road. He was a descendant of the historian of that name, who wrote one of the earliest accounts of the province. Peter was the most ancient inhabitant of the village, and well versed in all the wonderful events and traditions of the neighborhood. He recollected Rip at once, and corroborated his story in the most satisfactory manner. He assured the company that it was a fact, handed down from his ancestor the historian, that the Catskill Mountains had always been haunted by strange beings. That it was affirmed that the great Hendrick Hudson, the first discoverer of the river and country, kept a kind of vigil there every twenty years, with his crew of the *Half-moon;* being permitted in this way to revisit the scenes of his enterprise, and keep a guardian eye upon the river, and the great city called by his name.

That his father had once seen them in their old Dutch dresses playing at ninepins in a hollow of the mountain; and that he himself had heard, one summer afternoon, the sound of their balls, like distant peals of thunder.

To make a long story short, the company broke up, and returned to the more important concerns of the election. Rip's daughter took him home to live with her; she had a snug, well-furnished house, and a stout cheery farmer for a husband, whom Rip recollected for one of the urchins that used to climb upon his back. As to Rip's son and heir, who was the ditto of himself, seen leaning against the tree, he was employed to work on the farm; but evinced an hereditary disposition to attend to anything else but his business.

III

AT ABBOTSFORD WITH SCOTT[5]

I HAD a letter of introduction to him from Thomas Campbell the poet, and had reason to think, from the interest he had taken in some of my earlier scribblings,[6] that a visit from me would not be deemed an intrusion.

On the following morning, after an early breakfast, I set off in a post-chaise for the Abbey.

---

[5] From the collection of papers entitled "Crayon Miscellany." Irving's visit was made in 1817. His account of it was not published until nearly twenty years afterward—that is, after Scott's death.

[6] Irving at that time had published little more than the "Salmagundi" papers and "Knickerbocker's History of New York."

On the way thither I stopt at the gate of Abbotsford, and sent the postilion to the house with the letter of introduction and my card, on which I had written that I was on my way to the ruins of Melrose Abbey, and wished to know whether it would be agreeable to Mr. Scott (he had not yet been made a baronet) to receive a visit from me in the course of the morning. . . .

In a little while the "lord of the castle" himself made his appearance. I knew him at once by the descriptions I had read and heard, and the likeness that had been published of him. He was tall, and of a large and powerful frame. His dress was simple, and almost rustic: an old green shooting-coat, with a dog-whistle at the buttonhole, brown linen pantaloons, stout shoes that tied at the ankles, and a white hat that had evidently seen service. He came limping up the gravel-walk, aiding himself by a stout walking-staff, but moving rapidly and with vigor. By his side jogged along a large iron-gray stag-hound of most grave demeanor, who took no part in the clamor of the canine rabble, but seemed to consider himself bound, for the dignity of the house, to give me a courteous reception.

Before Scott had reached the gate he called out in a hearty tone, welcoming me to Abbotsford, and asking news of Campbell. Arrived at the door of the chaise, he grasped me warmly by the hand: "Come, drive down, drive down to the house," said he, "ye're just in time for breakfast, and afterward ye shall see all the wonders of the Abbey."

I would have excused myself, on the plea of having already made my breakfast. "Hout, man," cried he, "a ride in the morning in the keen air of the Scotch hills is warrant enough for a second breakfast." I was accordingly whirled to the portal of the cottage, and in a few moments found myself seated at the breakfast-table. . . .

Scott proposed a ramble to show me something of the surrounding country. As we sallied forth, every dog in the establishment turned out to attend us. There was the old stag-hound Maida, a noble animal, and a great favorite of Scott's; and Hamlet, the black greyhound, a wild thoughtless youngster, not yet arrived to the years of discretion; and Finette, a beautiful setter, with soft silken hair, long pendent ears, and a mild eye, the parlor favorite. When in front of the house, we were joined by a superannuated greyhound, who came from the kitchen wagging his tail, and was cheered by Scott as an old friend and comrade.

In our walks, Scott would frequently pause in conversation to notice his dogs and speak to them, as if rational companions; and, indeed, there appears to be a vast deal of rationality in these faithful attendants on man, derived from their close intimacy with him. Maida deported himself with a gravity becoming his age and size, and seemed to consider himself called upon to preserve a great degree of dignity and decorum in our society. As he jogged along a little distance ahead of us, the young dogs would gambol about him, leap on his neck, worry at his ears, and endeavor to tease him into a frolic. The old dog would keep on for a long time with imperturbable solemnity, now and then seeming to rebuke the wantonness of his young companions. . . .

We had not walked much further before we saw the two Miss Scotts advancing along the hillside to meet us. The morning's studies being over, they had set off to take a ramble on the hills, and gather heather-blossoms with which to decorate their hair for dinner. As they came bounding lightly, like young fawns, and their dresses fluttering in the pure summer breeze, I was reminded of Scott's own description of his children in his introduction to one of the cantos of "Marmion."

As they approached, the dogs all sprang forward and gamboled around them. They played with them for a time, and then joined us with countenances full of health and glee. Sophia,[7] the eldest, was the most lively and joyous, having much of her father's varied spirit in conversation, and seeming to catch excitement from his words and looks. Ann was of quieter mood, rather silent, owing, in some measure, no doubt, to her being some years younger.

At the dinner Scott had laid by his half-rustic dress, and appeared clad in black. The girls, too, in completing their toilet, had twisted in their hair the sprigs of purple heather which they had gathered on the hillside, and looked all fresh and blooming from their breezy walk.

There was no guest at dinner but myself. Around the table were two or three dogs in attendance. Maida, the old stag-hound, took his seat at Scott's elbow, looking up wistfully in his

[7] Sophia three years later became the wife of John Gibson Lockhart, the biographer of Scott.

master's eye, while Finette, the pet spaniel, placed herself near Mrs. Scott, by whom, I soon perceived, she was completely spoiled. . . .

Among the other important and privileged members of the household who figured in attendance at the dinner was a large gray cat, who, I observed, was regaled from time to time with titbits from the table. This sage grimalkin was a favorite of both master and mistress, and slept at night in their room; and Scott laughingly observed that one of the least wise parts of their establishment was that the window was left open at night for puss to go in and out. The cat assumed a kind of ascendency among the quadrupeds—sitting in state in Scott's armchair, and occasionally stationing himself on a chair beside the door, as if to review his subjects as they passed, giving each dog a cuff beside the ears as he went by. This clapper-clawing was always taken in good part; it appeared to be, in fact, a mere act of sovereignty on the part of grimalkin, to remind the others of their vassalage; which they acknowledged by the most perfect acquiescence. A general harmony prevailed between sovereign and subjects, and they would all sleep together in the sunshine. . . .

After dinner we adjourned to the drawing-room, which served also for study and library. Against the wall on one side was a long writing-table, with drawers; surmounted by a small cabinet of polished wood, with folding-drawers richly studded with brass ornaments, within which Scott kept his most valuable papers. Above the cabinet, in a kind of niche, was a complete corselet of glittering steel, with a closed helmet, and flanked by gantlets and battle-axes. Around were hung trophies and relics of various kinds; a simitar of Tipu Sahib; a Highland broadsword from Flodden field; a pair of Rippon spurs from Bannockburn, and above all, a gun which had belonged to Rob Roy, and bore his initials, R. M. C.,[8] an object of peculiar interest to me at the time, as it was understood Scott was actually engaged in printing a novel founded on the story of that famous outlaw.

On each side of the cabinet were bookcases, well stored with works of romantic fiction in various languages, many of them rare and antiquated. This, however, was merely his cottage library, the principal part of his books being at Edinburgh.

From this little cabinet of curiosities Scott drew forth a manuscript picked up on the field at Waterloo, containing copies of several songs popular at the time in France. The paper was dabbled with blood—"the very life-blood, very possibly," said Scott, "of some gay young officer who had cherished these songs as a keepsake from some lady-love in Paris." . . .

The evening passed away delightfully in this quaint-looking apartment, half study, half drawing-room. Scott had read several passages from the old romances of Arthur, with a fine deep sonorous voice, and a gravity of tone that seemed to suit the antiquated black-letter volume. It was a rich treat to hear such a work, read by such a person, and in such a place; and his appearance as he sat reading, in a large armed

[8] Robert McGregor Campbell was the real name of Rob Roy.

chair, with his favorite hound Maida at his feet and surrounded by books and relics, and border trophies, would have formed an admirable and most characteristic picture.

While Scott was reading, the sage grimalkin already mentioned had taken his seat in a chair beside the fire, and remained with fixt eye and grave demeanor, as if listening to the reader. I observed to Scott that his cat seemed to have a black-letter taste in literature.

"Ah," said he, "these cats are a very mysterious kind of folk. There is always more passing in their minds than we are aware of. It comes, no doubt, from their being so familiar with witches and warlocks." . . . .

When I retired for the night, I found it almost impossible to sleep; the idea of being under the roof of Scott, of being on the borders of the Tweed in the very center of that region which had for some time past been the favorite scene of romantic fiction, and above all, the recollections of the ramble I had taken, the company in which I had taken it, and the conversation which had passed, all fermented in my mind, and nearly drove sleep from my pillow.

On the following morning the sun darted his beams from over the hills through the low lattice window. I rose at an early hour, and looked out between the branches of eglantine which overhung the casement. To my surprize Scott was already up and forth, seated on a fragment of stone, and chatting with the workmen employed on the new building.[9] I had supposed, after the

[9] This "new building" became in time the mansion now known as Abbotsford. At the time of Irving's visit Scott

time he had wasted upon me yesterday, he would be closely occupied this morning; but he appeared like a man of leisure, who had nothing to do but bask in the sunshine and amuse himself.

I soon drest myself and joined him. He talked about his proposed plans of Abbotsford: happy would it have been for him could he have contented himself with his delightful little vine-covered cottage, and the simple yet hearty and hospitable style in which he lived at the time of my visit. The great pile of Abbotsford, with the huge expense it entailed upon him, of servants, retainers, guests, and baronial style, was a drain upon his purse, a tax upon his exertions, and a weight upon his mind, and finally crusht him. . . .

After breakfast Scott was occupied for some time correcting proof-sheets, which he had received by the mail. The novel of "Rob Roy,"[10] as I have already observed, was at that time in the press, and I supposed them to be the proof-sheets of that work. The authorship of the Waverley novels was still a matter of conjecture and uncertainty; tho few doubted their being principally written by Scott. One proof to me of his being the author was that he never adverted to them. A man so fond of anything Scottish, and anything relating to national history or local legend, could not have been mute

was living in a small villa which he had built after settling at the place in 1812. The present large castellated residence was produced by making extensive additions to the original villa.

[10] Of his novels Scott at this time had published only "Waverley," "Guy Mannering," "The Antiquarii" "Old Mortality" and the "Black Dwarf."

WASHINGTON IRVING

respecting such productions, had they been written by another. He was fond of quoting the works of his contemporaries; he was continually reciting scraps of border songs, or relating anecdotes of border story. With respect to his own poems and their merits, however, he was mute, and while with him I observed a scrupulous silence on the subject.

JAMES FENIMORE COOPER

Born in New Jersey in 1789, died in Cooperstown, N. Y., in 1851; son of William Cooper, the pioneer who founded Cooperstown; settled in Cooperstown in 1790; entered Yale College in 1803, remaining three years; midshipman in the navy in 1808; married in 1811 and resigned from the navy; published "Precaution" and "The Spy," both in 1821; the latter established his literary reputation; "The Pioneers" in 1823, "The Pilot" in 1823, "The Last of the Mohicans" in 1826; "The Prairie" in 1827, "The Pathfinder" in 1840, "The Deerslayer" in 1841; author of many other books.

I

HIS FATHER'S ARRIVAL AT OTSEGO LAKE[1]

NEAR the center of the State of New York lies an extensive district of country whose surface is a succession of hills and dales, or, to speak with greater deference to geographical definitions, of mountains and valleys. It is among these hills that the Delaware takes its rise; and,

[1] From Chapters I and III of "The Pioneers." Cooper's father, Judge William Cooper, the founder of Cooperstown, first visited Otsego Lake in 1785, built a house there in 1787 and in 1790 made it the permanent home of his family. In 1790 the place contained 35 other people. The selection here given pictures the circumstances in which Judge Cooper, as well as Marmaduke Temple, visited Otsego Lake. Fenimore Cooper was not two years old when his father settled there. His native place was Burlington, N. J.

JAMES FENIMORE COOPER

flowing from the limpid lakes and thousand springs of this region, the numerous sources of the Susquehanna meander through the valleys, until, uniting their streams, they form one of the proudest rivers of the United States. The mountains are generally arable to the tops, altho instances are not wanting where the sides are jutted with rocks, that aid greatly in giving to the country that romantic and picturesque character which it so eminently possesses.

The vales are narrow, rich and cultivated, with a stream uniformly winding through each. Beautiful and thriving villages are found interspersed along the margins of the small lakes, or situated at those points of the stream which are favorable for manufacturing; and neat and comfortable farms, with every indication of wealth about them, are scattered profusely through the vales, and even to the mountain tops. Roads diverge in every direction from the even and graceful bottoms of the valleys to the most rugged and intricate passes of the hills. Academies [2] and minor edifices of learning meet the eye of the stranger at every few miles as he winds his way through this uneven territory, and places for the worship of God abound with that frequency

---

Judge Cooper's settling at Cooperstown was a consequence of his having acquired, through foreclosure, extensive lands which George Croghan had failed in an attempt to settle, near the lake. Except for this circumstance, it is unlikely that his son ever would have acquired that intimate knowledge of Indian and frontier life of which he has left such notable pictures in his books.

[2] An "academy" was a high school or seminary, of which an example could be found as late as fifty years ago in almost every prosperous village of Central New York.

which characterizes a moral and reflecting people, and with that variety of exterior and canonical government which flows from unfettered liberty of conscience. . . .

It was near the setting of the sun, on a clear, cold day in December, when a sleigh was moving slowly up one of the mountains in the district we have described. The day had been fine for the season, and but two or three large clouds, whose color seemed brightened by the light reflected from the mass of snow that covered the earth, floated in a sky of the purest blue. The road wound along the brow of a precipice, and on one side was upheld by a foundation of logs, piled one upon the other, while a narrow excavation in the mountain in the opposite direction had made a passage of sufficient width for the ordinary traveling of that day. But logs, excavation, and everything that did not reach several feet above the earth lay alike buried beneath the snow. A single track, barely wide enough to receive the sleigh, denoted the route of the highway, and this was sunk nearly two feet below the surrounding surface.

In the vale, which lay at a distance of several hundred feet lower, there was what, in the language of the country, was called a clearing, and all the usual improvements of a new settlement; these even extended up the hill to the point where the road turned short and ran across the level land, which lay on the summit of the mountain; but the summit itself remained in the forest. There was glittering in the atmosphere, as if it was filled with innumerable shining particles; and the noble bay horses that drew the sleigh were covered, in many parts, with a coat of hoar-frost. The vapor from their nostrils was seen to issue like smoke; and every object in the view, as well as every arrangement of the travelers, denoted the depth of a winter in the mountains.

The harness, which was of a deep, dull black, differing from the glossy varnishing of the present day, was ornamented with enormous plates and buckles of brass, that shone like gold in those transient beams of the sun which found their way obliquely through the tops of the trees. Huge saddles, studded with nails and fitted with cloth that served as blankets to the shoulders of the cattle, supported four high, square-topped turrets, through which the stout reins led from the mouths of the horses to the hands of the driver, who was a negro of apparently twenty years of age. His face, which Nature had colored with a glistening black, was now mottled with the cold, and his large shining eyes filled with tears; a tribute to its power, that the keen frosts of those regions always extracted from one of his African origin. Still, there was a smiling expression of good humor in his happy countenance, that was created by the thoughts of home, and a Christmas fireside, with its Christmas frolics. . . .

A dark spot of a few acres in extent at the southern extremity of this beautiful flat, and immediately under the feet of our travelers, alone showed by its rippling surface, and the vapors which exhaled from it, that what at first might seem a plain was one of the mountain lakes, locked in the frosts of winter. A narrow current rushed impetuously from its bosom at the open place we mentioned and was to be traced for miles as it wound its way toward the south through the real valley, by its borders of hemlock and pine, and by the vapor which arose from its warmer surface into the chill atmosphere of the hills. The banks of this lovely basin, at its outlet,[3] or southern end, were steep, but not high; and in that direction the land continued, far as the eye could reach, a narrow but graceful valley, along which the settlers had scattered their humble habitations, with a profusion that bespoke the quality of the soil, and the comparative facilities of intercourse.

Immediately on the bank of the lake and at its foot stood the village of Templeton.[4] It consisted of some fifty buildings, including those of every description, chiefly built of wood, and which in their architecture bore no great marks of taste, but which also, by the unfinished appearance of most of the dwellings, indicated the hasty manner of their construction. To the eye they presented a variety of colors. A few were white in both front and rear, but more bore that expensive color on their fronts only, while their economical but ambitious owners had covered the remaining sides of the edifices with a dingy red. One or two were slowly assuming the russet of age; while the uncovered beams that were to be seen through the broken windows on their second stories showed that either the taste or the vanity of their proprietors had led them to

[3] The outlet of this lake is the Susquehanna River.
[4] Templeton is another name for Cooperstown.

undertake a task which they were unable to accomplish.

The whole were grouped in a manner that aped the streets of the city, and were evidently so arranged by the directions of one who looked to the wants of posterity rather than to the convenience of the present incumbents. Some three or four of the better sort of buildings, in addition to the uniformity of their color, were fitted with green blinds, which, at that season at least, were rather strangely contrasted to the chill aspect of the lake, the mountains, the forests, and the wide fields of snow. Before the doors of these pretentious dwellings were placed a few saplings, either without branches, or possessing only the feeble shoots of one or two summers' growth, that looked not unlike tall grenadiers on post near the threshold of princes. In truth, the occupants of these favored habitations were the nobles of Templeton, as Marmaduke was its king. They were the dwellings of two young men who were cunning in the law; an equal number of that class who chaffered to the wants of the community under the title of storekeepers; and a disciple of Æsculapius, who, for a novelty, brought more subjects into the world than he sent out of it.

In the midst of this incongruous group of dwellings rose the mansion of the Judge, towering above all its neighbors. It stood in the center of an enclosure of several acres, which was covered with fruit-trees. Some of the latter had been left by the Indians, and began already to assume the moss and inclination of age, therein forming a very marked contrast to the infant plantations that peered over most of the picketed fences of the village. In addition to this show of cultivation were two rows of young Lombardy poplars, a tree but lately introduced into America, formally lining either side of a pathway which led from a gate that opened on the principal street to the front door of the building. The house itself had been built entirely under the superintendence of a certain Mr. Richard Jones, whom we have already mentioned, and who, from his cleverness in small matters, and an entire willingness to exert his talents, added to the circumstances of their being sisters' children, ordinarily superintended all the minor concerns of Marmaduke Temple. Richard was fond of saying that this child of invention consisted of nothing more or less than what should form the groundwork of every clergyman's discourse, viz., a firstly and a lastly. He had commenced his labors, in the first year of their residence, by erecting a tall, gaunt edifice of wood, with its gable toward the highway. In this shelter, for it was little more, the family resided three years. By the end of that period Richard had completed his design. He had availed himself, in this heavy undertaking, of the experience of a certain wandering Eastern mechanic, who, by exhibiting a few soiled plates of English architecture, and talking learnedly of friezes, entablatures, and particularly of the composite order, had obtained a very undue influence over Richard's taste in everything that pertained to that branch of the fine arts. Not that Mr. Jones did not affect to consider Hiram Doolittle a perfect empiric in his profession, being in the constant habit of listening to his treatises on architecture with a kind of indulgent smile; yet, either from an inability to oppose them by anything plausible from his own stores of learning, or from secret admiration, Richard generally submitted to the arguments of his coadjutor.

Together they had not only directed a dwelling for Marmaduke, but they had given a fashion to the architecture of the whole country. The composite order, Mr. Doolittle would contend, was an order composed of many others, and was intended to be the most useful of all, for it admitted into its construction such alterations as convenience or circumstances might require. To this proposition Richard usually assented; and when rival geniuses, who monopolize not only all the reputation, but most of the money of the neighborhood, are of a mind, it is not uncommon to see them lead the fashion, even in graver matters. In the present instance, as we have already hinted, the castle, as Judge Temple's dwelling was termed in common parlance, came to be the model, in some one or other of its numerous excellences, for every aspiring edifice within twenty miles of it.[5]

[5] Judge Cooper's new home was called Otsego Hall. It was afterward improved by Fenimore Cooper and remained his home during the many years he spent in Cooperstown. A few years after his death it was destroyed by fire. Its site is now a village park.

II

RUNNING THE GANTLET[6]

Tho astonished at first by the uproar, Heyward was soon enabled to find its solution by the scene that followed. There yet lingered sufficient light in the heavens to exhibit those bright openings among the tree-tops where different paths left the clearing to enter the depths of the wilderness. Beneath one of them, a line of warriors issued from the woods and advanced slowly toward the dwellings. One in front bore a short pole, on which, as it afterward appeared, were suspended several human scalps. The startling sounds that Duncan had heard were what the whites have not inappropriately called the "death-hallo"; and each repetition of the cry was intended to announce to the tribe the fate of an enemy. Thus far the knowledge of Heyward assisted him in the explanation; and as he knew that the interruption was caused by the unlooked-for return of a successful war-party, every disagreeable sensation was quieted in inward congratulations for the opportune relief and insignificance it conferred on himself.

When at the distance of a few hundred feet from the lodges, the newly arrived warriors halted. The plaintive and terrific cry which was intended to represent equally the wailings of the dead and the triumph of the victors, had entirely ceased. One of their number now called aloud, in words that were far from appalling,

[6] From Chapter XXIII of "The Last of the Mohicans."

tho not more intelligible to those for whose ears they were intended than their expressive yells. It would be difficult to convey a suitable idea of the savage ecstasy with which the news thus imparted was received. The whole encampment in a moment became a scene of the most violent bustle and commotion. The warriors drew their knives, and flourishing them, they arranged themselves in two lines, forming a lane that extended from the war-party to the lodges. The squaws seized clubs, axes, or whatever weapons of offense first offered itself to their hands, and rushed eagerly to act their part in the cruel game that was at hand. Even the children would not be excluded; but boys, little able to wield the instruments, tore the tomahawks from the belts of their fathers, and stole into the ranks, apt imitators of the savage traits exhibited by their parents.

Large piles of brush lay scattered about the clearing, and a wary and aged squaw was occupied firing as many as might serve to light the coming exhibition. As the flame arose, its power exceeded that of the parting day, and assisted to render objects at the same time more distinct and more hideous. The whole scene formed a striking picture, whose frame was composed of the dark and tall border of pines. The warriors just arrived were the most distant figures. A little in advance stood two men, who were apparently selected from the rest as the principal actors in what was to follow. The light was not strong enough to render their features distinct, tho it was quite evident that they were governed by very different emotions. While one stood erect and firm, prepared to meet his fate like a hero, the other bowed his head, as if palsied by terror or stricken with shame.

The high-spirited Duncan felt a powerful impulse of admiration and pity toward the former, tho no opportunity could offer to exhibit his generous emotions. He watched his slightest movement, however, with eager eyes; and as he traced the fine outline of his admirably proportioned and active frame, he endeavored to persuade himself that if the powers of man, seconded by such noble resolution, could bear one harmless through so severe a trial, the youthful captive before him might hope for success in the hazardous race he was about to run. Insensibly the young man drew nigher to the swarthy lines of the Hurons, and scarcely breathed, so intense became his interest in the spectacle. Just then the signal yell was given, and the momentary quiet which had preceded it was broken by a burst of cries that far exceeded any before heard. The most abject of the two victims continued motionless; but the other bounded from the place at the cry, with the activity and the swiftness of a deer. Instead of rushing through the hostile lines as had been expected, he just entered the dangerous defile, and before time was given for a single blow, turned short, and leaping the heads of a row of children, he gained at once the exterior and safer side of the formidable array. The artifice was answered by a hundred voices raised in imprecations, and the whole of the excited multitude broke from their order and spread themselves about the place in wild confusion.

JAMES FENIMORE COOPER

A dozen blazing piles now shed their lurid brightness on the place, which resembled some unhallowed and supernatural arena in which malicious demons had assembled to act their bloody and lawless rites. The forms in the background looked like unearthly beings gliding before the eye and cleaving the air with frantic and unmeaning gestures; while the savage passions of such as passed the flames were rendered fearfully distinct by the gleams that shot athwart their inflamed visages.

It will easily be understood that amid such a concourse of vindictive enemies no breathing-time was allowed the fugitive. There was a single moment when it seemed as if he would have reached the forest; but the whole body of his captors threw themselves before him, and drove him back into the center of his relentless persecutors. Turning like a headed deer, he shot with the swiftness of an arrow through a pillar of forked flame, and passing the whole multitude harmless he appeared on the opposite side of the clearing. Here, too, he was met and turned by a few of the older and more subtle of the Hurons. Once more he tried the throng, as if seeking safety in its blindness; and then several moments succeeded, during which Duncan believed the active and courageous young stranger was lost.

Nothing could be distinguished but a dark mass of human forms tossed and involved in inexplicable confusion. Arms, gleaming knives, and formidable clubs appeared above them, but the blows were evidently given at random. The awful effect was heightened by the piercing shrieks of the women and the fierce yells of the warriors. Now and then Duncan caught a glimpse of a light form cleaving the air in some desperate bound, and he rather hoped than believed that the captive yet retained the command of his astonishing powers of activity. Suddenly the multitude rolled backward, and approached the spot where he himself stood. The heavy body in the rear prest upon the women and children in front, and bore them to the earth. The stranger reappeared in the confusion. Human power could not, however, much longer endure so severe a trial. . . .

There was no term of abuse known to the Huron vocabulary that the disappointed women did not lavishly expend on the successful stranger. They flouted at his efforts, and told him with bitter scoffs that his feet were better than his hands, and that he merited wings, while he knew not the use of an arrow or a knife. To all this the captive made no reply, but was content to preserve an attitude in which dignity was singularly blended with disdain. Exasperated as much by his composure as by his good fortune, their words became unintelligible, and were succeeded by shrill piercing yells. Just then the crafty squaw who had taken the necessary precautions to fire the piles made her way through the throng, and cleared a place for herself in front of the captive. The squalid and withered person of this hag might well have obtained for her the character of possessing more than human cunning. Throwing back her light vestment, she stretched forth her long skinny arm in derision, and using the language of the Lenape, as more intelligible to the subject of her gibes, she commenced aloud:

"Look you, Delaware," she said, snapping her fingers in his face, "your nation is a race of women, and the hoe is better fitted to your hands than the gun. Your squaws are the mothers of deer; but if a bear or a wild cat or a serpent were born among you, ye would flee. The Huron girls shall make you petticoats, and we will find you a husband."

A burst of savage laughter succeeded this attack, during which the soft and musical merriment of the younger females strangely chimed with the cracked voice of their older and more malignant companion. But the stranger was superior to all their efforts. His head was immovable, nor did he betray the slightest consciousness that any were present, except when his haughty eyes rolled toward the dusky forms of the warriors who stalked in the background, silent and sullen observers of the scene.

Infuriated at the self-command of the captive, the woman placed her arms akimbo, and throwing herself into a posture of defiance she broke out anew, in a torrent of words that no art of ours could commit successfully to paper. Her breath was, however, expended in vain; for, altho distinguished in her nation as a proficient in the art of abuse, she was permitted to work herself into such a fury as actually to foam at the mouth, without causing a muscle to vibrate in the motionless figure of the stranger. The effect of his indifference began to extend itself to the other spectators, and a youngster who was just quitting the condition of a boy to enter the state of manhood, attempted to assist the termagant by flourishing his tomahawk before their victim and adding his empty boasts to the taunts of the woman. Then, indeed, the captive turned his face toward the light, and looked down on the stripling with an expression that was superior to contempt. At the next moment he resumed his quiet and reclining attitude against the post. But the change of posture had permitted Duncan to exchange glances with the firm and piercing eyes of Uncas.

Breathless with amazement, and heavily opprest with the critical situation of his friend, Heyward recoiled before the look, trembling lest its meaning might in some unknown manner hasten the prisoner's fate. There was not, however, any instant cause for such an apprehension. Just then a warrior forced his way into the exasperated crowd. Motioning the women and children aside with a stern gesture, he took Uncas by the arm and led him toward the door of the council lodge. Thither all the chiefs and most of the distinguished warriors followed, among whom the anxious Heyward found means to enter without attracting any dangerous attention to himself.

A few minutes were consumed in disposing of those present in a manner suitable to their rank and influence in the tribe. An order very similar to that adopted in the preceding interview was observed, the aged and superior chiefs occupying the area of the spacious apartment, within the powerful light of a glaring torch, while their juniors and inferiors were arranged in the background, presenting a dark outline of swarthy and marked visages. In the very center of the lodge, immediately under an opening that admitted the twinkling light of one or two stars, stood Uncas, calm, elevated, and collected. His high and haughty carriage was not lost on his captors, who often bent their looks on his person with eyes which, while they lost none of their inflexibility of purpose, plainly betrayed their admiration of the stranger's daring.

III

LEATHER-STOCKING'S FAREWELL[7]

EFFINGHAM and Elizabeth were surprised at the manner of the Leather-Stocking, which was unusually impressive and solemn; but, attributing it to the scene, the young man turned to the monument, and read aloud:

"Sacred to the memory of Oliver Effingham, Esquire, formerly a major in his B. Majesty's 60th Foot; a soldier of tried valor; a subject of chivalrous loyalty; and a man of honesty. To these virtues he added the graces of a Christian.

[7] From Chapter XLI of "The Pioneers." Leather-Stocking was a name given by Cooper to his character Natty Bumppo, who, also, in various works, bore the name of Hawkeye, Pathfinder and Deerslayer. Leather-Stocking appears in five of Cooper's books, which are commonly and collectively known as "the Leather-Stocking Tales." He has generally been accepted as a type of the hardy frontiersman who, in the years following the Revolution, carried civilization westward.

The morning of his life was spent in honor, wealth, and power; but its evening was obscured by poverty, neglect, and disease, which were alleviated only by the tender care of his old, faithful, and upright friend and attendant, Nathaniel Bumppo. His descendants rear this stone to the virtues of the master, and to the enduring gratitude of the servant.''

The Leather-Stocking stared at the sound of his own name, and a smile of joy illumined his wrinkled features as he said:

"And did ye say it, lad? have you then got the old man's name cut in the stone by the side of his master's? God bless ye, children! 'twas a kind thought, and kindness goes to the heart as life shortens."

Elizabeth turned her back to the speakers. Effingham made a fruitless effort before he succeeded in saying:

"It is there cut in plain marble; but it should have been written in letters of gold!"

"Show me the name, boy," said Natty, with simple eagerness; "let me see my own name placed in such honor. 'Tis a gin'rous gift to a man who leaves none of his name and family behind him, in a country where he has tarried so long."

Effingham guided his finger to the spot, and Natty followed the windings of the letters to the end with deep interest, when he raised himself from the tomb, and said:

"I suppose it's all right; and it's kindly thought, and kindly done! But what have ye put over the redskin?"

"You shall hear:

"'This stone is raised to the memory of an Indian chief, of the Delaware tribe, who was known by the several names of John Mohegan; Mohican' "—

"Mo-hee-can, lad, they call theirselves! 'he-can."

"Mohican; 'and Chingagook' "—

" 'Gach, boy; 'gach-gook; Chingachgook, which, intarpreted, means Big Sarpent. The name should be set down right, for an Indian's name has always some meaning in it."

"I will see it altered. 'He was the last of his people who continued to inhabit this country; and it may be said of him that his faults were those of an Indian, and his virtues those of a man.' "

"You never said truer word, Mr. Oliver; ah's me! if you had knowed him as I did, in his prime, in that very battle where the old gentleman, who sleeps by his side, saved his life, when them thieves, the Iroquois, had him at the stake, you'd have said all that, and more too. I cut the thongs with this very hand, and gave him my own tomahawk and knife, seeing that the rifle was always my fav'rite weapon. He did lay about him like a man! I met him as I was coming home from the trail, with eleven Mingo scalps on his pole. You needn't shudder, Madam Effingham, for they was all from shaved heads and warriors. When I look about me, at these hills, where I used to count sometimes twenty smokes, curling over the tree-tops, from the Delaware camps, it raises mournful thoughts, to think that not a redskin is left of them all; unless it be a drunken vagabond from the Oneidas, or them Yankee Indians, who, they say, be moving up from the sea-shore; and who belong to none of God's creatures, to my seeming, being, as it were, neither fish nor flesh—neither white man nor savage. Well, well! the time has come at last, and I must go"—

"Go!" echoed Edwards, "whither do you go?"

The Leather-Stocking, who had imbibed, unconsciously, many of the Indian qualities, tho he always thought of himself as of a civilized being, compared with even the Delawares, averted his face to conceal the workings of his muscles, as he stooped to lift a large pack from behind the tomb, which he placed deliberately on his shoulders.

"Go!" exclaimed Elizabeth, approaching him with a hurried step; "you should not venture so far in the woods alone, at your time of life, Natty; indeed, it is imprudent. He is bent, Effingham, on some distant hunting."

"What Mrs. Effingham tells you is true, Leather-Stocking," said Edwards; "there can be no necessity for your submitting to such hardships now! So throw aside your pack, and confine your hunt to the mountains near us, if you will go."

"Hardship! 'tis a pleasure, children, and the greatest that is left me on this side the grave."

"No, no; you shall not go to such a distance," cried Elizabeth, laying her white hand on his deerskin pack; "I am right! I feel his camp-kettle, and a canister of powder! he must not be suffered to wander so far from us, Oliver; remember how suddenly Mohegan dropt away."

"I knowed the parting would come hard, chil-

JAMES FENIMORE COOPER

dren; I knowed it would!" said Natty, "and so I got aside to look at the graves by myself, and thought if I left ye the keepsake which the Major gave me, when we first parted in the woods, ye wouldn't take it unkind, but would know that, let the old man's body go where it might, his feeling stayed behind him."

"This means something more than common!" exclaimed the youth; "where is it, Natty, that you purpose going?"

The hunter drew nigh him with a confident, reasoning air, as if what he had to say would silence all objections, and replied:

"Why, lad, they tell me that on the Big Lakes there's the best of hunting, and a great range, without a white man on it, unless it may be one like myself. I'm weary of living in clearings, and where the hammer is sounding in my ears from sunrise to sundown. And tho I'm much bound to ye both, children—I wouldn't say it if it was not true—I crave to go into the woods ag'in, I do."

"Woods!" echoed Elizabeth, trembling with her feelings; "do you not call these endless forests woods?"

"Ah! child, these be nothing to a man that's used to the wilderness. I have took but little comfort sin' your father come on with his settlers; but I wouldn't go far, while the life was in the body that lies under the sod there. But now he's gone, and Chingachgook is gone; and you be both young and happy. Yes! the big house has rung with merriment this month past! And now, I thought, was the time to try to get a little comfort in the close of my days. Woods!

indeed! I doesn't call these woods, Madam Effingham, where I lose myself every day of my life in the clearings."

"If there be anything wanting to your comfort, name it, Leather-Stocking; if it be attainable it is yours."

"You mean all for the best, lad; I know it; and so does Madam, too: but your ways isn't my ways. 'Tis like the dead there, who thought, when the breath was in them, that one went east, and one went west to find their heavens; but they'll meet at last; and so shall we, children. Yes, ind as you've begun, and we shall meet in the land of the just at last."

"This is so new! so unexpected!" said Elizabeth, in almost breathless excitement; "I had thought you meant to live with us and die with us, Natty."

"Words are of no avail," exclaimed her husband; "the habits of forty years are not to be dispossest by the ties of a day. I know you too well to urge you further, Natty; unless you will let me build you a hut on one of the distant hills, where we can sometimes see you, and know that you are comfortable."

"Don't fear for the Leather-Stocking, children; God will see that his days be provided for, and his ind happy. I know you mean all for the best, but our ways doesn't agree. I love the woods, and ye relish the face of man; I eat when hungry, and drink when a-dry; and ye keep stated hours and rules: nay, nay, you even overfeed the dogs, lad, from pure kindness; and hounds should be gaunty to run well. The meanest of God's creatures be made for some use, and I'm formed for the wilderness; if ye love me, let me go where my soul craves to be ag'in!"

The appeal was decisive; and not another word of entreaty for him to remain was then uttered; but Elizabeth bent her head to her bosom and wept, while her husband dashed away the tears from his eyes; and, with hands that almost refused to perform their office, he produced his pocketbook, and extended a parcel of banknotes to the hunter.

"Take these," he said, "at least take these; secure them about your person, and in the hour of need they will do you good service."

The old man took the notes, and examined them with a curious eye.

"This, then, is some of the new-fashioned money that they've been making at Albany, out of paper! It can't be worth much to they that hasn't l'arning! No, no, lad—take back the stuff; it will do me no sarvice. I took kear to get all the Frenchman's powder afore he broke up, and they say lead grows where I'm going. It isn't even fit for wads, seeing that I use none but leather! Madam Effingham, let an old man kiss your hand, and wish God's choicest blessings on you and your'n."

"Once more let me beseech you, stay!" cried Elizabeth. "Do not, Leather-Stocking, leave me to grieve for the man who has twice rescued me from death, and who has served those I love so faithfully. For my sake, if not for your own, stay. I shall see you in those frightful dreams that still haunt my nights, dying in poverty and age, by the side of those terrific beasts you slew.

There will be no evil that sickness, want, and solitude can inflict that my fancy will not conjure as your fate. Stay with us, old man, if not for your own sake, at least for ours."

"Such thoughts and bitter dreams, Madam Effingham," returned the hunter, solemnly, "will never haunt an innocent parson long. They'll pass away with God's pleasure. And if the catamounts be yet brought to your eyes in sleep, 'tis not for my sake, but to show you the power of Him that led me there to save you. Trust in God, madam, and your honorable husband, and the thoughts for an old man like me can never be long nor bitter. I pray that the Lord will keep you in mind—the Lord that lives in clearings as well as in the wilderness—and bless you, and all that belong to you, from this time till the great day when the whites shall meet the redskins in judgment, and justice shall be the law, and not power."

Elizabeth raised her head, and offered her colorless cheek to his salute, when he lifted his cap and touched it respectfully. His hand was grasped with convulsive fervor by the youth, who continued silent. The hunter prepared himself for his journey, drawing his belt tighter, and wasting his moments in the little reluctant movements of a sorrowful departure. Once or twice he essayed to speak, but a rising in his throat prevented it. At length he shouldered his rifle, and cried with a clear huntsman's call that echoed through the woods:

"He-e-e-re, he-e-e-re, pups—away, dogs, away; ye'll be footsore afore ye see the ind of the journey!"

JAMES FENIMORE COOPER

The hounds leapt from the earth at this cry, and scenting around the graves and the silent pair, as if conscious of their own destination, they followed humbly at the heels of their master. A short pause succeeded, during which even the youth concealed his face on his grandfather's tomb. When the pride of manhood, however, had supprest the feelings of nature, he turned to renew his entreaties, but saw that the cemetery was occupied only by himself and his wife.

"He is gone!" cried Effingham.

Elizabeth raised her face, and saw the old hunter standing, looking back for a moment, on the verge of the wood. As he caught their glances, he drew his hard hand hastily across his eyes again, waved it on high for an adieu, and uttering a forced cry to his dogs, who were crouching at his feet, he entered the forest.

This was the last that they ever saw of the Leather-Stocking, whose rapid movements preceded the pursuit which Judge Temple both ordered and conducted. He had gone far toward the setting sun—the foremost in that band of pioneers who are opening the way for the march of the nation across the continent.

WILLIAM CULLEN BRYANT

Born in Massachusetts in 1794, died in New York in 1878; studied at Williams College in 1810-11; admitted to the bar in 1815; published "Thanatopsis" in 1816; a volume of "Poems" in 1821; joined the staff of the New York *Evening Post*, becoming its chief editor in 1829; published another volume of poems in 1832; opposed the extension of slavery; published a translation of Homer in 1870-71; his "Prose Writings" published after his death.

AN OCTOBER DAY IN FLORENCE[1]

WAKED by the jangling of all the bells in Florence and by the noise of carriages departing loaded with travelers for Rome and other places in the south of Italy, I rise, dress myself, and take my place at the window. I see crowds of men and women from the country, the former in brown velvet jackets, and the latter in broad-brimmed straw hats, driving donkeys loaded with panniers or trundling handcarts before them, heaped with grapes, figs and all the fruits of the orchard, the garden, and the field. They have hardly passed when large flocks of sheep and goats make their appearance, attended by shepherds and their families, driven by the approach

---

[1] From the "Letters of a Traveler," first published in book form in 1850. The selection here given was written in 1834. It has been republished by Parke Godwin, Bryant's biographer and editor, in one of his two volumes devoted to the "Prose Writings."

of winter from the Apenines, and seeking the pastures of the Maremma, a rich, but, in the summer, an unhealthy tract on the coast. The men and boys are drest in knee-breeches, the women in bodices, and both sexes wear capotes with pointed hoods, and felt hats with conical crowns; they carry long staves in their hands, and their arms are loaded with kids and lambs too young to keep pace with their mothers.

After the long procession of sheep and goats and dogs and men and women and children, come horses loaded with cloths and poles for tents, kitchen utensils, and the rest of the younglings of the flock. A little after sunrise I see well-fed donkeys, in coverings of red cloth, driven over the bridge to be milked for invalids. Maid-servants, bareheaded, with huge, high-carved combs in their hair, waiters of coffee-houses carrying the morning cup of coffee or chocolate to their customers, bakers' boys with a dozen loaves on a board balanced on their heads, milkmen with rush baskets filled with flasks of milk are crossing the streets in all directions. A little later the bell of the small chapel opposite to my window rings furiously for a quarter of an hour, and then I hear mass chanted in a deep strong nasal tone. As the day advances, the English, in white hats and white pantaloons, come out of their lodgings, accompanied sometimes by their hale and square-built spouses, and saunter stiffly along the Arno, or take their way to the public galleries and museums. Their massive, clean, and brightly polished carriages also begin to rattle through the streets, setting out on excursions to some part of the environs of Florence—to Fiesole, to the

Pratolino, to the Bello Sguardo, to the Poggio Imperiale.

Sights of a different kind now present themselves. Sometimes it is a troop of stout Franciscan friars, in sandals and brown robes, each carrying his staff and wearing a brown, broad-brimmed hat with a hemispherical crown. Sometimes it is a band of young theological students, in purple cassocks with red collars and cuffs, let out on a holiday, attended by their clerical instructors, to ramble in the Cascine. There is a priest coming over the bridge, a man of venerable age and great reputation for sanctity. The common people crowd around him to kiss his hand, and obtain a kind word from him as he passes. But what is that procession of men in black gowns, black gaiters, and black masks moving swiftly along, and bearing on their shoulders a litter covered with black cloth? These are the Brethren of Mercy, who have assembled at the sound of the cathedral bell, and are conveying some sick or wounded person to the hospital.

As the day begins to decline, the number of carriages in the streets, filled with gaily drest people attended by servants in livery, increases. The Grand Duke's equipage, an elegant carriage drawn by six horses, with coachmen, footmen, and outriders in drab-colored livery, comes from the Pitti Palace, and crosses the Arno, either by the bridge close to my lodgings, or by that called Alla Santa Trinita, which is in full sight from the windows. The Florentine nobility, with their families, and the English residents now throng to the Cascine, to drive at a slow pace through its thickly planted walks of elms, oaks and ilexes.

WILLIAM CULLEN BRYANT

As the sun is sinking I perceive the quay on the other side of the Arno filled with a moving crowd of well-drest people walking to and fro and enjoying the beauty of the evening.

Travelers now arrive from all quarters, in cabriolets, in calashes, in the shabby vettura, and in the elegant private carriage drawn by post-horses, and driven by postilions in the tightest possible deerskin breeches, the smallest red coats, and the hugest jack-boots. The streets about the doors of the hotels resound with the crackling of whips and the stamping of horses, and are encumbered with carriages, heaps of baggage, porters, postilions, couriers, and travelers. Night at length arrives—the time of spectacles and funerals. The carriages rattle toward the opera-houses. Trains of people, sometimes in white robes and sometimes in black, carrying blazing torches and a cross elevated on a high pole before a coffin, pass through the streets chanting the service for the dead. The Brethren of Mercy may also be seen engaged in their office. The rapidity of their pace, the flare of their torches, the gleam of their eyes through their masks, and their sable garb, give them a kind of supernatural appearance. I return to bed and fall asleep amidst the shouts of people returning from the opera, singing as they go snatches of the music with which they had been entertained during the evening.

WILLIAM H. PRESCOTT

Born in Salem, Mass., in 1796; died in Boston in 1859; studied at Harvard, where, through an accident to his eyes, he became nearly blind; devoted himself to the study of Spanish history, employing a reader and using a specially constructed writing apparatus; published his "Ferdinand and Isabella" in 1838; "Conquest of Mexico" in 1843, "Conquest of Peru" in 1847, and "Philip II" in 1855-58.

I

THE FATE OF EGMONT AND HOORNE[1]

ON the second of June, 1568, a body of three thousand men was ordered to Ghent to escort the Counts Egmont and Hoorne to Brussels. No resistance was offered, altho the presence of the Spaniards caused a great sensation among the inhabitants of the place, who too well foreboded the fate of their beloved lord.

The nobles, each accompanied by two officers, were put into separate chariots. They were guarded by twenty companies of pikemen and arquebusiers; and a detachment of lancers, among whom was a body of the duke's own horse, rode in the van, while another of equal strength protected the rear. Under this strong escort they moved slowly toward Brussels. One night they halted at Dendermonde, and toward evening, on

[1] From Book III, Chapter V, of the "History of the Reign of Philip II, King of Spain."

the fourth of the month, entered the capital. As the martial array defiled through its streets, there was no one, however stout-hearted he might be, says an eye-witness, who could behold the funeral pomp of the procession, and listen to the strains of melancholy music without a feeling of sickness at his heart.

The prisoners were at once conducted to the *Brod-huys*, or "Bread-house," usually known as the *Maison du Roi*—that venerable pile in the market-place of Brussels, still visited by every traveler for its curious architecture, and yet more as the last resting-place of the Flemish lords. Here they were lodged in separate rooms, small, dark, and uncomfortable, and scantily provided with furniture. Nearly the whole of the force which had escorted them to Brussels was established in the great square, to defeat any attempt at a rescue. But none was made; and the night passed away without disturbance, except what was occasioned by the sound of busy workmen employed in constructing a scaffold for the scene of execution on the following day.

On the afternoon of the fourth, the Duke of Alva[2] had sent for Martin Rithovius, bishop of Ypres; and, communicating to him the sentence of the nobles, he requested the prelate to visit the prisoners, acquaint them with their fate, and prepare them for their execution on the following day. The bishop, an excellent man, and the per-

---

[2] The Duke of Alva was sent to the Netherlands as governor in 1567 where, as an instrument of his cruelty, he established what is known as "The Council of Blood," a court of inquiry and persecution which, in the course of three months, put to death 1,600 persons.

sonal friend of Egmont, was astounded by the tidings. He threw himself at Alva's feet, imploring mercy for the prisoners, and if he could not spare their lives, beseeching him at least to grant them more time for preparation. But Alva sternly rebuked the prelate, saying that he had been summoned not to thwart the execution of the law, but to console the prisoners and enable them to die like Christians. The bishop, finding his entreaties useless, rose and addrest himself to his melancholy mission.

It was near midnight when he entered Egmont's apartment, where he found the poor nobleman, whose strength had been already reduced by confinement, and who was wearied by the fatigue of the journey, buried in slumber. It is said that the two lords, when summoned to Brussels, had indulged the vain hope that it was to inform them of the conclusion of their trial and their acquittal! However this may be, Egmont seems to have been but ill prepared for the dreadful tidings he received. He turned deadly pale as he listened to the bishop, and exclaimed, with deep emotion, "It is a terrible sentence. Little did I imagine that any offense I had committed against God or the king could merit such punishment. It is not death that I fear. Death is the common lot of all. But I shrink from dishonor. Yet I may hope that my sufferings will so far expiate my offenses that my innocent family will not be involved in my ruin by the confiscation of my property. This much, at least, I think I may claim in consideration of my past services." Then, after a pause, he added, "Since my death is the will of God and his Majesty, I will try to meet it with patience." He asked the bishop if there were no hope. On being answered, "None whatever," he resolved to devote himself at once to preparing for the solemn change.

He rose from his couch, and hastily drest himself. He then made his confession to the prelate, and desired that mass might be said, and the sacrament administered to him. This was done with great solemnity, and Egmont received the communion in the most devout manner, manifesting the greatest contrition for his sins. He next inquired of the bishop to what prayer he could best have recourse to sustain him in this trying hour. The prelate recommended to him that prayer which our Savior had commended to his disciples. The advice pleased the count, who earnestly engaged in his devotions. But a host of tender recollections crowded on his mind, and the images of his wife and children drew his thoughts in another direction, till the kind expostulations of the prelate again restored him to himself.

Egmont asked whether it would be well to say anything on the scaffold for the edification of the people. But the bishop discouraged him, saying that he would be imperfectly heard, and that the people, in their present excitement, would be apt to misinterpret what he said to their own prejudice.

Having attended to his spiritual concerns, Egmont called for writing materials, and wrote a letter to his wife, whom he had not seen during his long confinement; and to her he now bade a tender farewell. He then addrest another letter, written in French, in a few brief and touching sentences, to the King—which fortunately has been preserved to us. "This morning," he says, "I have been made acquainted with the sentence which it has pleased your majesty to pass upon me. And altho it has never been my intent to do aught against the person or the service of your majesty, or against our true, ancient, and Catholic faith, yet I receive in patience what it has pleased God to send me. If during these troubles I have counseled or permitted aught which might seem otherwise, I have done so from a sincere regard for the service of God and your majesty, and from what I believed the necessity of the times. Wherefore I pray your majesty to pardon it, and for the sake of my past services to take pity on my poor wife, my children, and my servants. In this trust I commend myself to the mercy of God." The letter is dated Brussels, "on the point of death," June 5th, 1568.

Having time still left, the count made a fair copy of the two letters, and gave them to the bishop, entreating him to deliver them according to their destination. He accompanied that to Philip with a ring, to be given at the same time to the monarch. It was of great value, and, as it had been the gift of Philip himself during the count's late visit to Madrid, it might soften the heart of the King by reminding him of happier days, when he had looked with an eye of favor on his unhappy vassal.

Having completed all his arrangements, Egmont became impatient for the hour of his departure; and he exprest the hope that there would be no unnecessary delay. At ten in the morning the soldiers appeared who were to conduct him to the scaffold. They brought with them cords, as usual, to bind the prisoner's hands. But Egmont remonstrated, and showed that he had himself cut off the collar of his doublet and shirt, in order to facilitate the stroke of the executioner. This he did to convince them that he meditated no resistance; and on his promising that he would attempt none, they consented to his remaining with his hands unbound.

Egmont was drest in a crimson damask robe, over which was a Spanish mantle fringed with gold. His breeches were of black silk, and his hat, of the same material, was garnished with white and sable plumes. In his hand, which, as we have seen, remained free, he held a white handkerchief. On his way to the place of execution he was accompanied by Julian de Romero, *maître de camp*, by the captain, Salinas, who had charge of the fortress of Ghent, and by the bishop of Ypres. As the procession moved slowly forward, the count repeated some portion of the fifty-first Psalm—"Have mercy on me, O God!"—in which the good prelate joined with him. In the center of the square, on the spot where so much of the best blood of the Netherlands had been shed, stood the scaffold, covered with black cloth. On it were two velvet cushions with a small table, shrouded likewise in black, and supporting a silver crucifix. At the corners of the platform were two poles, pointed at the end with steel, intimating the purpose for which they were intended.

In front of the scaffold was the provost of the court, mounted on horseback, and bearing the red wand of office in his hand. The executioner remained, as usual, below the platform, screened from view, that he might not, by his presence before it was necessary, outrage the feelings of the prisoners. The troops, who had been under arms all night, were drawn up around in order of battle; and strong bodies of arquebusiers were posted in the great avenues which led to the square. The space left open by the soldiery was speedily occupied by a crowd of eager spectators. Others thronged the roofs and windows of the buildings that surrounded the market-place, some of which, still standing at the present day, show, by their quaint and venerable architecture, that they must have looked down on the tragic scene we are now depicting.

It was indeed a gloomy day for Brussels—so long the residence of the two nobles, where their forms were as familiar and where they were held in as much love and honor as in any of their own provinces. All business was suspended. The shops were closed. The bells tolled in all the churches. An air of gloom, as of some impending calamity, settled on the city. "It seemed," says one residing there at the time, "as if the day of judgment were at hand!"

As the procession slowly passed through the ranks of the soldiers, Egmont saluted the officers —some of them his ancient companions—with such a sweet and dignified composure in his manner as was long remembered by those who saw it. And few even of the Spaniards could refrain from tears as they took their last look at the gallant noble who was to perish so miserably.

WILLIAM H. PRESCOTT

With a steady step he mounted the scaffold, and, as he crossed it, gave utterance to the vain wish that, instead of meeting such a fate, he had been allowed to die in the service of his King and country. He quickly, however, turned to other thoughts, and, kneeling on one of the cushions, with the bishop beside him on the other, he was soon engaged earnestly in prayer. With his eyes raised toward heaven with a look of unutterable sadness, he prayed so fervently and loud as to be distinctly heard by the spectators. The prelate, much affected, put into his hands the silver crucifix, which Egmont repeatedly kissed; after which, having received absolution for the last time, he rose and made a sign to the bishop to retire. He then stript off his mantle and robe; and, again kneeling, he drew a silk cap, which he had brought for the purpose, over his eyes, and, repeating the words, "Into Thy hands, O Lord, I commend my spirit," he calmly awaited the stroke of the executioner.

The low sounds of lamentation which from time to time had been heard among the populace were now hushed into silence as the minister of justice, appearing on the platform, approached his victim and with a single blow of the sword severed the head from the body. A cry of horror rose from the multitude, and some, frantic with grief, broke through the ranks of the soldiers and wildly dipped their handkerchiefs in the blood that streamed from the scaffold, treasuring them up, says the chronicler, as precious memorials of love and incitements to vengeance. The head was then set on one of the poles at the end of the platform, while a mantle thrown over the mutilated trunk hid it from the public gaze.

It was near noon when orders were sent to lead forth the remaining prisoner to execution. It had been assigned to the curate of La Chapelle to acquaint Count Hoorne with his fate. That nobleman received the awful tidings with less patience than was shown by his friend. He gave way to a burst of indignation at the cruelty and injustice of the sentence. It was a poor requital, he said, for eight-and-twenty years of faithful service to his sovereign. Yet, he added, he was not sorry to be released from a life of such incessant fatigue. For some time he refused to confess, saying he had done enough in the way of confession. When urged not to throw away the few precious moments that were left to him, he at length consented.

The count was drest in a plain suit of black, and wore a Milanese cap upon his head. He was, at this time, about fifty years of age. He was tall, with handsome features, and altogether of a commanding presence. His form was erect, and as he passed with a steady step through the files of soldiers, on his way to the place of execution, he frankly saluted those of his acquaintance whom he saw among the spectators. His look had in it less of sorrow than of indignation, like that of one conscious of enduring wrong. He was spared one pang, in his last hour, which had filled Egmont's cup with bitterness; tho, like him, he had a wife, he was to leave no orphan family to mourn him.

As he trod the scaffold, the apparatus of death seemed to have no power to move him. He still repeated the declaration that, "often as he had offended his Maker, he had never, to his knowledge, committed any offense against the King." When his eyes fell on the bloody shroud that enveloped the remains of Egmont, he inquired if it were the body of his friend. Being answered in the affirmative, he made some remark in Castilian, not understood. He then prayed for a few moments, but in so low a tone that the words were not caught by the bystanders, and, rising, he asked pardon of those around if he had ever offended any of them, and earnestly besought their prayers. Then, without further delay, he knelt down, and, repeating the words, "*In manus tuas, Domine,*" he submitted himself to his fate.

His bloody head was set up opposite to that of his fellow sufferer. For three hours these ghastly trophies remained exposed to the gaze of the multitude. They were then taken down, and, with the bodies, placed in leaden coffins, which were straightway removed—that containing the remains of Egmont to the convent of Santa Clara, and that of Hoorne to the ancient church of Ste. Gudule. To these places, especially to Santa Clara, the people now flocked as to the shrine of a martyr. They threw themselves on the coffin, kissing it and bedewing it with their tears, as if it had contained the relics of some murdered saint; while many of them, taking little heed of the presence of informers, breathed vows of vengeance, some even swearing not to trim either hair or beard till these vows were executed. The government seems to have thought it prudent to take no notice of this burst of popular feeling. But a funeral hatchment, blazoned with the arms of Egmont, which, as usual after the master's death, had been fixt by his domestics on the gates of his mansion, was ordered to be instantly removed—no doubt, as tending to keep alive the popular excitement. The bodies were not allowed to remain long in their temporary places of deposit, but were transported to the family residences of the two lords in the country, and laid in the vaults of their ancestors.

Thus by the hand of the common executioner perished these two unfortunate noblemen, who, by their rank, possessions, and personal characters, were the most illustrious victims that could have been selected in the Netherlands. Both had early enjoyed the favor of Charles the Fifth, and both had been entrusted by Philip with some of the highest offices in the state. Philip de Montmorency, Count Hoorne, the elder of the two, came of the ancient house of Montmorency in France. Besides filling the high post of Admiral of the Low Countries, he was made governor of the provinces of Guelders and Zutphen, was a councilor of state, and was created by the Emperor a knight of the Golden Fleece. His fortune was greatly inferior to that of Count Egmont; yet its confiscation afforded a supply by no means unwelcome to the needy exchequer of the Duke of Alva.

However nearly on a footing they might be in many respects, Hoorne was altogether eclipsed by his friend in military renown.

WILLIAM H. PRESCOTT

II

THE GENESIS OF "DON QUIXOTE"[2]

THE age of chivalry, as depicted in romances, could never, of course, have had any real existence; but the sentiments which are described as animating that age have been found more or less operative in different countries and different periods of society. In Spain, especially, this influence is to be discerned from a very early date. Its inhabitants may be said to have lived in a romantic atmosphere, in which all the extravagances of chivalry were nourished by their peculiar situation. Their hostile relations with the Moslem kept alive the full glow of religious and patriotic feeling. Their history is one interminable crusade. An enemy always on the borders invited perpetual displays of personal daring and adventure. The refinement and magnificence of the Spanish Arabs throw a luster over these contests such as could not be reflected from the rude skirmishes with their Christian neighbors. Lofty sentiments, embellished by the softer refinements of courtesy, were blended in the martial bosom of the Spaniard, and Spain became emphatically the land of romantic chivalry.

The very laws themselves, conceived in this

[2] From the "Biographical and Critical Miscellanies," which were collected by the author for publication in England in 1845. This essay, and the others in the volume, with one exception, had been published originally in *The North American Review*.

spirit, contributed greatly to foster it. The ancient code of Alfonso X, in the thirteenth century, after many minute regulations for the deportment of the good knight, enjoins on him to "invoke the name of his mistress in the fight, that it may infuse new ardor into his soul and preserve him from the commission of unknightly actions." Such laws were not a dead letter. The history of Spain shows that the sentiment of romantic gallantry penetrated the nation more deeply and continued longer than in any other quarter of Christendom. . . .

The taste for these romantic extravagances naturally fostered a corresponding taste for the perusal of tales of chivalry. Indeed, they acted reciprocally on each other. These chimerical legends had once, also, beguiled the long evenings of our Norman ancestors, but, in the progress of civilization, had gradually given way to other and more natural forms of composition. They still maintained their ground in Italy, whither they had passed later, and where they were consecrated by the hand of genius. But Italy was not the true soil of chivalry, and the inimitable fictions of Bojardo, Pulci, and Ariosto were composed with that lurking smile of half-supprest mirth which, far from a serious tone, could raise only a corresponding smile of incredulity in the reader.

In Spain, however, the marvels of romance were all taken in perfect good faith. Not that they were received as literally true; but the reader surrendered himself up to the illusion, and was moved to admiration by the recital of deeds which, viewed in any other light than as a wild frolic of imagination, would be supremely ridiculous; for these tales had not the merit of a seductive style and melodious versification to relieve them. They were, for the most part, an ill-digested mass of incongruities, in which there was as little keeping and probability in the characters as in the incidents, while the whole was told in that stilted "Hercles' vein" and with that licentiousness of allusion and imagery which could not fail to debauch both the taste and the morals of the youthful reader. The mind, familiarized with these monstrous, over-colored pictures, lost all relish for the chaste and sober productions of art. The love of the gigantic and the marvelous indisposed the reader for the simple delineations of truth in real history. . . .

Cervantes brought forward a personage, in whom were embodied all those generous virtues which belong to chivalry; disinterestedness, contempt of danger, unblemished honor, knightly courtesy, and those aspirations after ideal excellence which, if empty dreams, are the dreams of a magnanimous spirit. They are, indeed, represented by Cervantes as too ethereal for this world, and are successively dispelled as they come in contact with the coarse realities of life. It is this view of the subject which has led Sismondi, among other critics, to consider that the principal end of the author was "the ridicule of enthusiasm—the contrast of the heroic with the vulgar"—and he sees something profoundly sad in the conclusions to which it leads. This sort of criticism appears to be over-refined. It resembles the efforts of some commentators to allegorize the great epics of Homer and Virgil, throwing a disagreeable mistinesss over the story by converting mere shadows into substances, and substances into shadows.

The great purpose of Cervantes was, doubtless, that expressly avowed by himself, namely, to correct the popular taste for romances of chivalry. It is unnecessary to look for any other in so plain a tale, altho, it is true, the conduct of the story produces impressions on the reader, to a certain extent, like those suggested by Sismondi. The melancholy tendency, however, is in a great degree counteracted by the exquisitely ludicrous character of the incidents. Perhaps, after all, if we are to hunt for a moral as the key of the fiction, we may with more reason pronounce it to be the necessity of proportioning our undertakings to our capacities.

The mind of the hero, Don Quixote, is an ideal world into which Cervantes has poured all the rich stores of his own imagination, the poet's golden dreams, high romantic exploit, and the sweet visions of pastoral happiness; the gorgeous chimeras of the fancied age of chivalry, which had so long entranced the world; splendid illusions, which, floating before us like the airy bubbles which the child throws off from his pipe, reflect, in a thousand variegated tints, the rude objects around, until, brought into collision with these, they are dashed in pieces and melt into air. These splendid images derive tenfold beauty from the rich antique coloring of the author's language, skilfully imitated from the old romances, but which necessarily escapes in the translation into a foreign tongue. Don Quixote's insanity operates both in mistaking the ideal for the real, and the real for the ideal. Whatever he has found in romances he believes to exist in the world; and he converts all he meets with in the world into the visions of his romances. It is difficult to say which of the two produces the most ludicrous results.

For the better exposure of these mad fancies Cervantes has not only put them into action in real life, but contrasted them with another character which may be said to form the reverse side of his hero's. Honest Sancho represents the material principle as perfectly as his master does the intellectual or ideal. He is of the earth, earthy. Sly, selfish, sensual, his dreams are not of glory, but of good feeding. His only concern is for his carcass. His notions of honor appear to be much the same with those of his jovial contemporary Falstaff, as conveyed in his memorable soliloquy. In the sublime night-piece which ends with the fulling-mills—truly sublime until we reach the dénouement—Sancho asks his master: "Why need you go about this adventure? It is main dark, and there is never a living soul sees us; we have nothing to do but to sheer off and get out of harm's way. Who is there to take notice of our flinching?" Can anything be imagined more exquisitely opposed to the true spirit of chivalry? The whole compass of fiction nowhere displays the power of contrast so forcibly as in these two characters; perfectly opposed to each other, not only in their minds and general habits, but in the minutest details of personal appearance.

It was a great effort of art for Cervantes to maintain the dignity of his hero's character in the midst of the whimsical and ridiculous distresses in which he has perpetually involved him. His infirmity leads us to distinguish between his character and his conduct, and to absolve him from all responsibility for the latter. The author's art is no less shown in regard to the other principal figure in the piece, Sancho Panza, who, with the most contemptible qualities, contrives to keep a strong hold on our interest by the kindness of his nature and his shrewd understanding. He is far too shrewd a person, indeed, to make it natural for him to have followed so crackbrained a master unless bribed by the promise of a substantial recompense. He is a personification, as it were, of the popular wisdom—a "bundle of proverbs," as his master somewhere styles him; and proverbs are the most compact form in which the wisdom of a people is digested. They have been collected into several distinct works in Spain, where they exceed in number those of any other, if not every other country in Europe. As many of them are of great antiquity, they are of inestimable price with the Castilian jurists, as affording rich samples of obsolete idioms and the various mutations of the language.

"Don Quixote" may be said to form an epoch in the history of letters, as the original of that kind of composition, the novel of character, which is one of the distinguishing peculiarities of modern literature. When well executed, this sort of writing rises to the dignity of history itself, and may be said to perform no insignificant part of the functions of the latter. History describes men less as they are than as they appear, as they are playing a part on the great political theater—men in masquerade. It rests on state documents, which too often cloak real purposes under an artful veil of policy, or on the accounts of contemporaries blinded by passion or interest. Even without these deductions, the revolutions of states, their wars, and their intrigues do not present the only aspect, nor, perhaps, the most interesting, under which human nature can be studied. It is man in his domestic relations, around his own fireside, where alone his real character can be truly disclosed; in his ordinary occupations in society, whether for purposes of profit or pleasure; in his every-day manner of living, his tastes and opinions, as drawn out in social intercourse; it is, in short, under all those forms which make up the interior of society that man is to be studied, if we would get the true form and pressure of the age—if, in short, we would obtain clear and correct ideas of the actual progress of civilization.

But these topics do not fall within the scope of the historian. He can not find authentic materials for them. They belong to the novelist, who, indeed, contrives his incidents and creates his characters, but who, if true to his art, animates them with the same tastes, sentiments, and motives of action which belong to the period of his fiction. His portrait is not the less true because no individual has sat for it. He has seized the physiognomy of the times. Who is there that does not derive a more distinct idea of the state of society and manners in Scotland from the "Waverley Novels" than from the best of its historians? Of the condition of the Middle

Ages from the single romance of "Ivanhoe" than from the volumes of Hume or Hallam? In like manner, the pencil of Cervantes has given a far more distinct and a richer portraiture of life in Spain in the sixteenth century than can be gathered from a library of monkish chronicles.

GEORGE BANCROFT

Born in Massachusetts in 1800; died in Washington in 1891; graduated from Harvard in 1817; studied in Germany; taught Greek in Harvard; established a private school at Northampton in 1823; collector of the Port of Boston in 1838; unsuccessful candidate for Governor of Massachusetts in 1844; Secretary of the Navy in 1845; established the Naval Academy at Annapolis; minister to England in 1846; minister to Berlin in 1867; published his "History of the United States" in 10 volumes in 1834-74.

THE FATE OF EVANGELINE'S COUNTRYMEN[1]
(1755)

THEY [the French inhabitants of Acadia] still counted in their villages "eight thousand" souls, and the English not more than "three thousand"; they stood in the way of "the progress of the settlement"; "by their non-compliance with

[1] From Volume IV, Chapter VIII, of "The History of the United States," as published in 1862. Acadia was the name of the original French colony in the eastern part of Canada, including Nova Scotia, New Brunswick and adjacent islands. It was first colonized by the French in 1604. It is more particularly of the French settlers in Nova Scotia that Bancroft writes. These were deported by the British in 1755. Longfellow's poem "Evangeline" is founded on an incident in this deportation, by which two lovers were hopelessly parted. Hawthorne is said first to have heard this story and considered it as the theme for a novel, but, unable to use it satisfactorily to himself, he passed it on to Longfellow.

the conditions of the treaty of Utrecht they had forfeited their possessions to the crown"; after the departure "of the fleet and troops, the province would not be in a condition to drive them out." "Such a juncture as the present might never occur"; so he [the chief justice, Belcher] advised "against receiving any of the French inhabitants to take the oath," and for the removal of "all" of them from the province.

That the cruelty might have no palliation, letters arrived leaving no doubt that the shores of the Bay of Fundy were entirely in the possession of the British; and yet at a council, at which Vice-Admiral Boscawen and Rear-Admiral Mostyn were present by invitation, it was unanimously determined to send the French inhabitants out of the province; and, after mature consideration, it was further unanimously agreed that, to prevent their attempting to return and molest the settlers that were to be set down on their lands, it would be most proper to distribute them among the several colonies on the continent.

To hunt them into the net was impracticable; artifice was therefore resorted to. By a general proclamation, on one and the same day, the scarcely conscious victims, "both old men and young men, as well as all the lads of ten years of age," were peremptorily ordered to assemble at their respective posts. On the appointed fifth of September they obeyed. At Grand Pré, for example, four hundred and eighteen unarmed men came together. They were marched into the church and its avenues were closed, when Winslow, the American commander, placed himself in their center, and spoke:

GEORGE BANCROFT

"You are convened together to manifest to you his majesty's final resolution to the French inhabitants of this his province. Your lands and tenements, cattle of all kinds, and live stock of all sorts, are forfeited to the crown, and you yourselves are to be removed from this his province. I am, through his majesty's goodness, directed to allow you liberty to carry off your money and household goods, as many as you can, without discommoding the vessels you go in."

And he then declared them the King's prisoners. Their wives and families shared their lot; their sons, five hundred and twenty-seven in number; their daughters, five hundred and seventy-six; in the whole, women and babes and old men and children all included, nineteen hundred and twenty-three souls. The blow was sudden; they had left home but for the morning, and they never were to return. Their cattle were to stay unfed in the stalls, their fires to die out on their hearths. They had for that first day even no food for themselves or their children, and were compelled to beg for bread.

The tenth of September was the day for the embarkation of a part of the exiles. They were drawn up six deep; and the young men, one hundred and sixty-one in number, were ordered to march first on board the vessel. They could leave their farms and cottages, the shady rocks on which they had reclined, their herds, and their garners; but nature yearned within them, and they would not be separated from their parents. Yet of what avail was the frenzied despair of the unarmed youth? They had not one weapon; the bayonet drove them to obey; and they marched slowly and heavily from the chapel to the shore, between women and children, who, kneeling, prayed for blessings on their heads, they themselves weeping and praying and singing hymns. The seniors went next; the wives and children must wait till other transport vessels arrive. The delay had its horrors. The wretched people left behind were kept together near the sea, without proper food, or raiment, or shelter, till other ships came to take them away; and December, with its appalling cold, had struck the shivering, half-clad, broken-hearted sufferers, before the last of them were removed.

"The embarkation of the inhabitants goes on but slowly," wrote Monckton, from Fort Cumberland, near which he had burned three hamlets; "the most part of the wives of the men we have prisoners are gone off with their children, in hopes I would not send off their husbands without them." Their hope was vain. Near Annapolis a hundred heads of families fled to the woods, and a party was detached on the hunt to bring them in. "Our soldiers hate them," wrote an officer on this occasion; "and, if they can but find a pretext to kill them, they will." Did a prisoner seek to escape, he was shot down by the sentinel. Yet some fled to Quebec; more than three thousand had withdrawn to Miramachi and the region south of the Restigouche; some found rest on the banks of the St. John's and its branches; some found a lair in their native forests; some were charitably sheltered from the English in the wigwams of the savages. But seven thousand of these banished people were driven on board ships, and

GEORGE BANCROFT

scattered among the British colonies, from New Hampshire to Georgia—one thousand and twenty to South Carolina alone. They were cast ashore without resources, hating the poorhouse as a shelter for their offspring, and abhorring the thought of selling themselves as laborers. Households, too, were separated; the colonial newspapers contained advertisements of members of families seeking their companions, of sons anxious to reach and relieve their parents, of mothers moaning for their children.

The wanderers sighed for their native country; but, to prevent their return, their villages, from Annapolis to the isthmus, were laid waste. Their old homes were but ruins. In the district of Minas, for instance, two hundred and fifty of their houses, and more than as many barns, were consumed. The live stock which belonged to them, consisting of great numbers of horned cattle, hogs, sheep, and horses, were seized as spoils and disposed of by the English officials. A beautiful and fertile tract of country was reduced to a solitude. There was none left round the ashes of the cottages of the Acadians but the faithful watch-dog, vainly seeking the hands that fed him. Thickets of forest-trees choked their orchards; the ocean broke over their neglected dikes, and desolated their meadows.

Relentless misfortune pursued the exiles wherever they fled. Those sent to Georgia, drawn by a love for the spot where they were born, as strong as that of the captive Jews who wept by the rivers of Babylon for their own temple and land, escaped to sea in boats, and went coasting from harbor to harbor; but when they had reached New England, just as they would have set sail for their native fields, they were stopt by orders from Nova Scotia. Those who dwelt on the St. John's were torn from their new homes. When Canada surrendered, hatred with its worst venom pursued the fifteen hundred who remained south of the Restigouche. Once those who dwelt in Pennsylvania presented a humble petition to the Earl of Loudoun, then the British commander-in-chief in America; and the cold-hearted peer, offended that the prayer was made in French, seized their five principal men, who in their own land had been persons of dignity and substance, and shipped them to England, with the request that they might be kept from ever again becoming troublesome by being consigned to service as common sailors on board ships-of-war. No doubt existed of the King's approbation. The lords of trade, more merciless than the savages and than the wilderness in winter, wished very much that every one of the Acadians should be driven out; and, when it seemed that the work was done, congratulated the King that "the zealous endeavors of Lawrence had been crowned with an entire success."

RALPH WALDO EMERSON

Born in 1803, died in 1882, a Unitarian clergyman in Boston in 1829-32; began a long career as lecturer in 1833; settled in Concord in 1834; editor of *The Dial* in 1842-44; published "Nature" in 1836; "Essays," two series, in 1841-44; "Poems" in 1846; "Representative Men" in 1850; "English Traits" in 1856; "Conduct of Life" in 1860; "Society and Solitude" in 1870; "Letters and Social Aims" in 1876.

I

THOREAU'S BROKEN TASK[1]

His robust common sense, armed with stout hands, keen perceptions, and strong will, can not yet account for the superiority which shone in his simple and hidden life. I must add the cardinal fact that there was an excellent wisdom in him, proper to a rare class of men, which showed him the material world as a means and symbol. This discovery, which sometimes yields to poets a certain casual and interrupted light, serving for the ornament of their writing, was in him an unsleeping insight; and whatever faults or obstructions of temperament might cloud it, he was not disobedient to the heavenly vision. In his youth he said one day, "The other world

[1] From Emerson's address at the funeral of Thoreau, as expanded for the *Atlantic Monthly* of August, 1862; usually printed since as an introduction to Thoreau's volume entitled "Excursions," published by Houghton, Mifflin & Company.

is all my art: my pencils will draw no other; my jack-knife will cut nothing else; I do not use it as a means." This was the muse and genius that ruled his opinions, conversation, studies, work and course of life. This made him a searching judge of men. At first glance he measured his companion, and, tho insensible to some fine traits of culture, could very well report his weight and caliber. And this made the impression of genius which his conversation often gave.

I think his fancy for referring everything to the meridian of Concord did not grow out of any ignorance or depreciation of other longitudes or latitudes, but was rather a playful expression of his conviction of the indifferency of all places, and that the best place for each is where he stands. He exprest it once in this wise: "I think nothing is to be hoped from you, if this bit of mold under your feet is not sweeter to you to eat than any other in this world, or in any world."

The other weapon with which he conquered all obstacles in science was patience. He knew how to sit immovable, a part of the rock he rested on, until the bird, the reptile, the fish, which had retired from him, should come back, and resume his habits, nay, moved by curiosity, should come to him and watch him.

It was a pleasure and a privilege to walk with him. He knew the country like a fox or a bird, and passed through it as freely by paths of his own. He knew every track in the snow or on the ground, and what creature had taken this path before him. One must submit abjectly to

RALPH WALDO EMERSON

such a guide, and the reward was great. Under his arm he carried an old music-book to press plants; in his pocket his diary and pencil, a spy-glass for birds, microscope, jack-knife, and twine. He wore straw hat, stout shoes, strong gray trousers, to brave shrub-oaks and smilax, and to climb a tree for a hawk's or a squirrel's nest. He waded into the pool for the water-plants, and his strong legs were no insignificant part of his armor.

No college ever offered him a diploma, or a professor's chair; no academy made him its corresponding secretary, its discoverer, or even its member. Perhaps these learned bodies feared the satire of his presence. Yet so much knowledge of Nature's secret and genius few others possest, none in a more large and religious synthesis. For not a particle of respect had he to the opinions of any man or body of men, but homage solely to the truth itself; and as he discovered everywhere among doctors some leaning of courtesy, it discredited them. He grew to be revered and admired by his townsmen, who had at first known him only as an oddity. The farmers who employed him as a surveyor soon discovered his rare accuracy and skill, his knowledge of their lands, of trees, of birds, of Indian remains, and the like, which enabled him to tell every farmer more than he knew before of his own farm; so that he began to feel as if Mr. Thoreau had better rights in his land than he. They felt, too, the superiority of character which addrest all men with a native authority.

His virtues, of course, sometimes ran into extremes. It was easy to trace to the inexorable demand on all for exact truth that austerity which made this willing hermit more solitary even than he wished. Himself of a perfect probity, he required not less of others. He had a disgust for crime, and no worldly success could cover it. He detected paltering as readily in dignified and prosperous persons as in beggars, and with equal scorn. Such dangerous frankness was in his dealing that his admirers called him "that terrible Thoreau," as if he spoke when silent, and was still present when he had departed. I think the severity of his ideal interfered to deprive him of a healthy sufficiency of human society.

The habit of a realist to find things the reverse of their appearance inclined him to put every statement in a paradox. A certain habit of antagonism defaced his earlier writings—a trick of rhetoric not quite outgrown in his later, of substituting for the obvious word and thought its diametrical opposite. He praised wild mountains and winter forests for their domestic air, in snow and ice he would find sultriness, and commended the wilderness for resembling Rome and Paris. "It was so dry that you might call it wet."

The tendency to magnify the moment, to read all the laws of Nature in the one object or one combination under your eye, is of course comic to those who do not share the philosopher's perception of identity. To him there was no such thing as size. The pond was a small ocean; the Atlantic a large Walden Pond. He referred every minute fact to cosmical laws. Tho he meant to be just, he seemed haunted by a certain chronic assumption that the science of the day pretended completeness, and he had just found out that the savants had neglected to discriminate a particular botanical variety, had failed to describe the seeds or count the sepals. "That is to say," we replied, "the blockheads were not born in Concord; but who said they were? It was their unspeakable misfortune to be born in London, or Paris, or Rome; but, poor fellows, they did what they could, considering that they never saw Bateman's Pond, or Nine-acre Corner, or Becky Stow's Swamp. Besides, what were you sent into the world for but to add this observation?"

Had this genius been only contemplative, he had been fitted to his life, but with his energy and practical ability he seemed born for great enterprise and for command; and I so much regret the loss of his rare powers of action that I can not help counting it a fault in him that he had no ambition. Wanting this, instead of engineering for all America, he was the captain of a huckleberry party. Pounding beans is good to the end of pounding empires one of these days; but if, at the end of years, it is still only beans!

But these foibles, real or apparent, were fast vanishing in the incessant growth of a spirit so robust and wise, and which effaced its defeats with new triumphs. His study of nature was a perpetual ornament to him, and inspired his friends with curiosity to see the world through his eyes, and to hear his adventures. They possest every kind of interest.

He had many elegances of his own, while he scoffed at conventional elegance. Thus, he could not bear to hear the sound of his own steps, the grit of gravel; and therefore never willingly walked in the road, but in the grass, on mountains and in woods. His senses were acute, and he remarked that by night every dwelling-house gives out bad air, like a slaughter-house. He liked the pure fragrance of melilot. He honored certain plants with special regard, and, over all, the pond lily, then the gentian, and the *Mikania scandens*, and "life-everlasting," and a bass-tree which he visited every year when it bloomed, in the middle of July. He thought the scent a more oracular inquisition than the sight—more oracular and trustworthy. The scent, of course, reveals what it concealed from the other senses. By it he detected earthiness. He delighted in echoes, and said they were almost the only kind of kindred voices that he heard. He loved Nature so well, was so happy in her solitude, that he became very jealous of cities, and the sad work which their refinements and artifices made with man and his dwelling. The ax was always destroying his forest. "Thank God," he said, "they can not cut down the clouds!" . . .

The scale on which his studies proceeded was so large as to require longevity, and we were the less prepared for his sudden disappearance. The country knows not yet, or in the least part, how great a son it has lost. It seems an injury that he should leave in the midst his broken task, which none else can finish—a kind of indignity to so noble a soul, that it should depart out of Nature before yet he has been really shown to his peers for what he is. But he, at least, is content. His soul was made for the noblest society; he had in a short life exhausted the capabilities of this world; wherever there is knowledge, wherever there is virtue, wherever there is beauty, he will find a home.

II

THE INTELLECTUAL HONESTY OF MONTAIGNE[2]

A SINGLE odd volume of Cotton's translation of the Essays remained to me from my father's library, when a boy. It lay long neglected, until, after many years, when I was newly escaped from college, I read the book, and procured the remaining volumes. I remember the delight and wonder in which I lived with it. It seemed to me as if I had myself written the book, in some former life, so sincerely it spoke to my thought and experience. It happened, when in Paris, in 1833, that, in the cemetery of Pere le Chaise, I came to a tomb of August Collignon, who died in 1830, aged sixty-eight years, and who, said the monument, "lived to do right, and had formed himself to virtue on the Essays of Montaigne." Some years later, I became acquainted with an accomplished English poet, John Sterling; and, in prosecuting my correspondence, I found that, from a love of Montaigne, he had made a pilgrimage to his chateau, still standing near Castellan, in Perigord, and, after two hundred and fifty years, had copied from the walls

[2] From "Montaigne; or The Skeptic," in "Representative Men." Published by Houghton, Mifflin & Company.

of his library the inscriptions which Montaigne had written there. That Journal of Mr. Sterling's, published in the *Westminster Review*, Mr. Hazlitt has reprinted in the Prolegomena to his edition of the Essays. I heard with pleasure that one of the newly-discovered autographs of William Shakespeare was in a copy of Florio's translation of Montaigne. It is the only book which we certainly know to have been in the poet's library. And, oddly enough, the duplicate copy of Florio, which the British Museum purchased with a view of protecting the Shakespeare autograph (as I was informed in the Museum), turned out to have the autograph of Ben Jonson in the fly-leaf. Leigh Hunt relates of Lord Byron that Montaigne was the only great writer of past times whom he read with avowed satisfaction. Other coincidences, not needful to be mentioned here, concurred to make this old Gascon still new and immortal for me.

In 1571, on the death of his father, Montaigne, then thirty-eight years old, retired from the practise of law at Bordeaux, and settled himself on his estate. Tho he had been a man of pleasure, and sometimes a courtier, his studious habits now grew on him, and he loved the compass, staidness, and independence of the country gentleman's life. He took up his economy in good earnest, and made his farms yield the most. Downright and plain-dealing, and abhorring to be deceived or to deceive, he was esteemed in the country for his sense and probity. In the civil wars of the League, which converted every house into a fort, Montaigne kept his gates open, and his house without defense. All parties freely came and went, his courage and honor being universally esteemed. The neighboring lords and gentry brought jewels and papers to him for safe-keeping. Gibbon reckons, in these bigoted times, but two men of liberality in France — Henry IV and Montaigne.

III

HIS VISIT TO CARLYLE AT CRAIGEN-PUTTOCK[2]
(1833)

FROM Edinburgh I went to the Highlands. On my return I came from Glasgow to Dumfries, and being intent on delivering a letter which I had brought from Rome, inquired for Craigenputtock. It was a farm in Nithsdale, in the parish of Dunscore, sixteen miles distant. No public coach passed near it, so I took a private carriage from the inn. I found the house amid desolate heathery hills, where the lonely scholar nourished his mighty heart. Carlyle was a man from his youth, an author who did not need to hide from his readers, and as absolute a man of the world, unknown and exiled on that hill-farm, as if holding on his own terms what is best in

[2] From Chapter I of "English Traits," published by Houghton, Mifflin Company. At the time of this visit, Emerson had published none of his books, but Carlyle was known as the author of many of the "Essays" now included among his collected writings, and had published the "Life of Schiller" and his translation of Goethe's "Wilhelm Meister." "Sartor Resartus" in that year was beginning its course through the monthly numbers of *Fraser's Magazine*.

London. He was tall and gaunt, with cliff-like brow, self-possest, and holding his extraordinary powers of conversation in easy command; clinging to his northern accent with evident relish; full of lively anecdote, and with a streaming humor, which floated everything he looked upon. His talk playfully exalting the familiar objects, put the companion at once into an acquaintance with his Lars and Lemurs, and it was very pleasant to learn what was predestined to be a pretty mythology. Few were the objects and lonely the man, "not a person to speak to within sixteen miles except the minister of Dunscore"; so that books inevitably made his topics.

He had names of his own for all the matters familiar to his discourse. *Blackwood's* was the "sand magazine"; *Fraser's* nearer approach to possibility of life was the "mud magazine"; a piece of road near by that marked some failed enterprise was the "grave of the last sixpence." When too much praise of any genius annoyed him, he profest hugely to admire the talent shown by his pig. He had spent much time and contrivance in confining the poor beast to one enclosure in his pen, but pig, by great strokes of judgment, had found out how to let a board down, and had foiled him. For all that, he still thought man the most plastic little fellow in the planet, and he liked Nero's death, "*Qualis artifex pereo!*" better than most history. He worships a man that will manifest any truth to him. At one time he had inquired and read a good deal about America. Landor's principle was mere rebellion, and *that* he feared was the American principle. The best thing he knew of that country was that in it a man can have meat for his labor. He had read in Stewart's book that, when he inquired in a New York hotel for the Boots, he had been shown across the street and had found Mungo in his own house dining on roast turkey.

We talked of books. Plato he does not read, and he disparaged Socrates; and, when prest, persisted in making Mirabeau a hero. Gibbon he called the splendid bridge from the old world to the new. His own reading had been multifarious. "Tristram Shandy" was one of his first books after "Robinson Crusoe," and Robertson's "America" an early favorite. Rousseau's "Confessions" had discovered to him that he was not a dunce; and it was now ten years since he had learned German, by the advice of a man who told him he would find in that language what he wanted.

He took despairing or satirical views of literature at this moment; recounted the incredible sums paid in one year by the great booksellers for puffing. Hence it comes that no newspaper is trusted now, no books are bought, and the booksellers are on the eve of bankruptcy.

He still returned to English pauperism, the crowded country, the selfish abdication by public men of all that public persons should perform. "Government should direct poor men what to do. Poor Irish folk come wandering over these moors. My dame makes it a rule to give to every son of Adam bread to eat, and supplies his wants to the next house. But here are thousands of acres which might give them all meat, and nobody to bid these poor Irish go to the moor and till it. They burned the stacks, and so found a way to force the rich people to attend to them."

We went out to walk over long hills, and looked at Criffel, then without his cap, and down into Wordsworth's country. There we sat down, and talked of the immortality of the soul. It was not Carlyle's fault that we talked on that topic, for he had the natural disinclination of every nimble spirit to bruise itself against walls, and did not like to place himself where no step can be taken. But he was honest and true, and cognizant of the subtile links that bind ages together, and saw how every event affects all the future. "Christ died on the tree: that built Dunscore kirk yonder: that brought you and me together. Time had only a relative existence."

He was already turning his eyes toward London with a scholar's appreciation. London is the heart of the world, he said, wonderful only from the mass of human beings. He liked the huge machine. Each keeps its own round. The baker's boy brings muffins to the window at a fixt hour every day, and that is all the Londoner knows or wishes to know on the subject. But it turned out good men. He named certain individuals, especially one man of letters, his friend, the best mind he knew, whom London had well served.

NATHANIEL HAWTHORNE

Born in Salem, Mass., in 1804; died in 1864; graduated from Bowdoin College in 1825; served in the Custom House in Boston; joined the Brook Farm community in 1841; surveyor of the port of Salem in 1846-49; consul at Liverpool in 1853-57; published "Fanshawe" at his own expense in 1826, "Twice Told Tales" in 1837-42; "Mosses from an Old Manse" in 1846, "The Scarlet Letter" in 1850, "House of the Seven Gables" in 1851, "The Marble Faun" in 1860, "Our Old Home" in 1863.

I

OCCUPANTS OF AN OLD MANSE[1]

BETWEEN two tall gate-posts of rough-hewn stone (the gate itself having fallen from its hinges at some unknown epoch) we beheld the gray front of the old parsonage terminating the vista of an avenue of black-ash trees. It was now a twelvemonth since the funeral procession of the venerable clergyman, its last inhabitant, had turned from that gateway toward the village burying-ground. The wheel track leading to the door, as well as the whole breadth of the avenue, was almost overgrown with grass, affording dainty mouthfuls to two or three vagrant cows and

[1] From the introductory chapter of "Mosses from an Old Manse," published by Houghton, Mifflin Company. This house, built in 1765, is still standing in Concord. Emerson lived there while writing his "Nature." Hawthorne made it his home soon after his marriage in 1842.

an old white horse who had his own living to pick up along the roadside. The glimmering shadows that lay half asleep between the door of the house and the public highway were a kind of spiritual medium, seen through which the edifice had not quite the aspect of belonging to the material world. Certainly, it had little in common with those ordinary abodes which stand so imminent upon the road that every passer-by can thrust his head, as it were, into the domestic circle. From these quiet windows the figures of passing travelers look too remote and dim to disturb the sense of privacy. In its near retirement and accessible seclusion, it was the very spot for the residence of a clergyman—a man not estranged from human life, yet enveloped, in the midst of it, with a veil woven of intermingled gloom and brightness. It was worthy to have been one of the time-honored parsonages of England, in which through many generations a succession of holy occupants pass from youth to age, and bequeath each an inheritance of sanctity to pervade the house and hover over it as with an atmosphere.

Nor, in truth, had the Old Manse ever been profaned by a lay occupant until that memorable summer afternoon when I entered it as my home. A priest had built it; a priest had succeeded to it; other priestly men from time to time had dwelt in it; and children born in its chambers had grown up to assume the priestly character. It was awful to reflect how many sermons must have been written there. The latest inhabitant alone—he by whose translation to paradise the dwelling was left vacant—had penned nearly three thousand discourses, besides the better if not the greater number that gushed living from his lips. How often, no doubt, had he paced to and fro along the avenue, attuning his meditations to the sighs and gentle murmurs and deep and solemn peals of the wind among the tops of the lofty trees! In that variety of natural utterances he could find something accordant with every passage of his sermon, were it of tenderness or reverential fear. The boughs over my head seemed shadowy with solemn thoughts, as well as with rustling leaves.

I took shame to myself for having been so long a writer of idle stories, and ventured to hope that wisdom would descend upon me with the falling leaves of the avenue, and that I should light upon an intellectual treasure in the Old Manse well worth those hoards of long-hidden gold which people seek for in moss-grown houses. Profound treatises of morality, a layman's unprofessional and therefore unprejudiced views of religion, histories (such as Bancroft might have written had he taken up his abode here, as he once proposed) bright with picture, gleaming over a depth of philosophic thought—these were the works that might fitly have flowed from such a retirement. In the humblest event, I resolved at least to achieve a novel that should evolve some deep lesson, and should possess physical substance enough to stand alone. . . .

The study had three windows set with little old-fashioned panes of glass, each with a crack across it. The two on the western side looked or rather peeped between the willow branches down into the orchard, with glimpses of the river through the trees. The third, facing northward, commanded a broader view of the river at a spot where its hitherto obscure waters gleam forth into the light of history. It was at this window that the clergyman who then dwelt in the manse stood watching the outbreak of a long and deadly struggle between two nations.[2] He saw the irregular array of his parishioners on the farther side of the river, and the glittering line of the British on the hither bank; he awaited in an agony of suspense the rattle of the musketry. It came; and there needed but a gentle wind to sweep the battle smoke around this quiet house. . . .

When summer was dead and buried, the Old Manse became as lonely as a hermitage. Not that ever—in my time at least—it had been thronged with company; but at no rare intervals we welcomed some friend out of the dusty glare and tumult of the world, and rejoiced to share with him the transparent obscurity that was floating over us. In one respect our precincts were like the Enchanted Ground through which the pilgrim traveled on his way to the Celestial City. The guests, each and all, felt a slumbrous influence upon them; they fell asleep in chairs, or took a more deliberate siesta on the sofa, or were seen stretched among the shadows of the orchard, looking up dreamily through the boughs. They could not have paid a more acceptable compliment to my abode, nor to my own qualities as a host. I held it as a proof that they left their cares behind them as they passed between

[2] The bridge at Concord, where the battle of April, 1775, was fought, stands only a short distance from the old manse.

the stone gate-posts at the entrance of our avenue, and that the so powerful opiate was the abundance of peace and quiet within and all around us. . . .

Hobgoblins of flesh and blood were attracted thither by the wide-spreading influence of a great original thinker, who had his earthly abode at the opposite extremity of our village. His mind acted upon other minds of a certain constitution with wonderful magnetism, and drew many men upon long pilgrimages to speak with him face to face. Young visionaries, to whom just so much of insight had been imparted as to make life all a labyrinth around them, came to seek the clue that should guide them out of their self-involved bewilderment. Gray-headed theorists, whose systems, at first air, had finally imprisoned them in an iron framework, traveled painfully to his door, not to ask deliverance, but to invite the free spirit into their own thraldom. People that had lighted on a new thought, or a thought that they fancied new, came to Emerson, as the finder of a glittering gem hastens to a lapidary to ascertain its quality and value. Uncertain, troubled, earnest wanderers through the midnight of a moral world beheld its intellectual fire as a beacon burning on a hill-top, and climbing the difficult ascent, looked forth into the surrounding obscurity more hopefully than hitherto. The light revealed objects unseen before—mountains, gleaming lakes, glimpses of a creation among the chaos; but also. as was unavoidable, it attracted bats and owls and the whole host of night birds, which flapped their dusky wings against the gazer's eyes, and sometimes were mistaken for fowls of angelic feather. Such delusions always hover nigh whenever a beacon-fire of truth is kindled.

For myself, there had been epochs of my life when I too might have asked of this prophet the master word that should solve me the riddle of the universe; but now, being happy, I felt as if there were no question to be put, and therefore admired Emerson as a poet of deep beauty and austere tenderness, but sought nothing from him as a philosopher. It was good nevertheless to meet him in the wood paths, or sometimes in our avenue, with that pure intellectual gleam diffused about his presence like the garment of a Shining One; and he so quiet, so simple, so without pretension, encountering each man alike as if expecting to receive more than he could impart. And in truth, the heart of many an ordinary man had, perchance, inscriptions which he could not read.

But it was impossible to dwell in his vicinity without inhaling more or less the mountain atmosphere of his lofty thought, which in the brains of some people wrought a singular giddiness—new truth being as heady as new wine. Never was a poor little country village infested with such a variety of queer, strangely drest, oddly behaved mortals, most of whom took upon themselves to be important agents of the world's destiny, yet were simply bores of a very intense water. Such, I imagine, is the invariable character of persons who crowd so closely about an original thinker as to draw in his unuttered breath, and thus to become imbued with a false originality. This triteness of novelty is enough to make any man of common sense blaspheme at all ideas of less than a century's standing, and pray that the world may be petrified and rendered immovable in precisely the worst moral and physical state that it ever yet arrived at, rather than be benefited by such schemes of such philosophers. . . .

Glancing back over what I have written, it seems but the scattered reminiscences of a single summer. In fairyland there is no measurement of time; and in a spot so sheltered from the turmoil of life's ocean, three years hasten away with a noiseless flight, as the breezy sunshine chases the cloud shadows across the depths of a still valley. Now came hints, growing more and more distinct, that the owner of the old house was pining for his native air. Carpenters next appeared, making a tremendous racket among the outbuildings, strewing the green grass with pine shavings and chips of chestnut joists, and vexing the whole antiquity of the place with their discordant renovations. Soon, moreover, they divested our abode of the veil of woodbine which had crept over a large portion of its southern face. All the aged mosses were cleared unsparingly away, and there were horrible whispers about brushing up the external walls with a coat of paint—a purpose as little to my taste as might be that of rouging the venerable cheeks of one's grandmother. But the hand that renovates is always more sacrilegious than that which destroys. In fine, we gathered up our household goods, drank a farewell cup of tea in our pleasant little breakfast-room—delicately fragrant tea, an unpurchasable luxury, one of the many angel gifts that had fallen like dew upon us—and passed forth between the tall stone gate-posts, as uncertain as the wandering Arabs where our tent might next be pitched. Providence took me by the hand, and—an oddity of dispensation which, I trust, there is no irreverence in smiling at—has led me, as the newspapers announce, while I am writing from the Old Manse, into a custom-house.[3] As a story-teller I have often contrived strange vicissitudes for my imaginary personages, but none like this.

II

ARTHUR DIMMESDALE ON THE SCAFFOLD[4]

THE crowd was in a tumult. The men of rank and dignity, who stood more immediately around the clergyman, were so taken by surprize, and so perplexed as to the purport of what they saw —unable to receive the explanation which most readily presented itself, or to imagine any other— that they remained silent and inactive spectators of the judgment which Providence seemed about to work. They beheld the minister, leaning on Hester's shoulder, and supported by her arm around him, approach the scaffold, and ascend its steps; while still the little hand of the sin-born child was clasped in his. Old Roger Chill-

---

[3] A reference to his appointment to a position in the Boston Custom-house.
[4] From Chapters XIII and XIV of "The Scarlet Letter," published by Houghton, Mifflin & Company.

ingworth followed, as one intimately connected with the drama of guilt and sorrow in which they had all been actors, and well entitled, therefore, to be present at its closing scene.

"Hadst thou sought the whole earth over," said he, looking darkly at the clergyman, "there was no one place so secret—no high place nor lowly place, where thou couldst have escaped me—save on this very scaffold!"

"Thanks be to Him who hath led me hither!" answered the minister.

Yet he trembled, and turned to Hester with an expression of doubt and anxiety in his eyes, not the less evidently betrayed that there was a feeble smile upon his lips.

"Is not this better," murmured he, "than what we dreamed of in the forest?"

"I know not! I know not!" she hurriedly replied. "Better? Yea; so we may both die, and little Pearl die with us!"

"For thee and Pearl, be it as God shall order," said the minister; "and God is merciful! Let me now do the will which He hath made plain before my sight. For, Hester, I am a dying man. So let me make haste to take my shame upon me!"

Partly supported by Hester Prynne, and holding one hand of little Pearl's, the Reverend Mr. Dimmesdale turned to the dignified and venerable rulers; to the holy ministers, who were his brethren; to the people, whose great heart was thoroughly appalled, yet overflowing with tearful sympathy, as knowing that some deep life-matter —which, if full of sin, was full of anguish and repentance likewise—was now to be laid open to them. The sun, but little past its meridian, shone down upon the clergyman, and gave a distinctness to his figure as he stood out from all the earth to put in his plea of guilty at the bar of Eternal Justice.

"People of New England!" cried he, with a voice that rose over them, high, solemn, and majestic—yet had always a tremor through it, and sometimes a shriek, struggling up out of a fathomless depth of remorse and wo—"ye that have loved me!—ye that have deemed me holy!—behold me here, the one sinner of the world! At last!—at last!—I stand upon the spot where, seven years since, I should have stood; here, with this woman, whose arm, more than the little strength wherewith I have crept hitherward, sustains me, at this dreadful moment, from groveling down upon my face! Lo, the scarlet letter which Hester wears! Ye have all shuddered at it! Wherever her walk hath been—wherever, so miserably burdened, she may have hoped to find repose—it hath cast a lurid gleam of awe and horrible repugnance round about her. But there stood one in the midst of you, at whose brand of sin and infamy ye have not shuddered!"

It seemed, at this point, as if the minister must leave the remainder of his secret undisclosed. But he fought back the bodily weakness—and, still more, the faintness of heart—that was striving for the mastery with him. He threw off all assistance, and stept passionately forward a pace before the woman and the child.

"It was on him!" he continued, with a kind of fierceness—so determined was he to speak out the whole. "God's eye beheld it! The angels were forever pointing at it! The devil knew it well, and fretted it continually with the touch of his burning finger! But he hid it cunningly from men, and walked among you with the mien of a spirit, mournful, because so pure in a sinful world—and sad, because he missed his heavenly kindred! Now, at the death-hour, he stands up before you! He bids you look again at Hester's scarlet letter! He tells you that, with all its mysterious horror, it is but the shadow of what he bears on his own breast, and that even this, his own red stigma, is no more than the type of what has seared his inmost heart! Stand any here that question God's judgment on a sinner? Behold! Behold a dreadful witness of it!''

With a convulsive motion, he tore away the ministerial band from his breast. It was revealed! But it were irreverent to describe that revelation. For an instant the gaze of the horror-stricken multitude was concentrated on the ghastly miracle; while the minister stood, with a flush of triumph in his face, as one who, in the crisis of acutest pain, had won a victory. Then, down he sank upon the scaffold! Hester partly raised him, and supported his head against her bosom. Old Roger Chillingworth knelt down beside him, with a blank, dull countenance, out of which the life seemed to have departed.

"Thou hast escaped me!" he repeated more than once. "Thou hast escaped me!"

"May God forgive thee!" said the minister. "Thou, too, hast deeply sinned!"

He withdrew his dying eyes from the old man, and fixt them on the woman and the child.

"My little Pearl," said he, feebly—and there was a sweet and gentle smile over his face, as of a spirit sinking into deep repose; nay, now that the burden was removed, it seemed almost as if he would be sportive with the child—"dear little Pearl, wilt thou kiss me now? Thou wouldst not yonder, in the forest! But now thou wilt?"

Pearl kissed his lips. A spell was broken. The great scene of grief, in which the wild infant bore a part, had developed all her sympathies; and as her tears fell upon her father's cheek, they were the pledge that she would grow up amid human joy and sorrow, nor forever do battle with the world, but be a woman in it. Toward her mother, too, Pearl's errand as a messenger of anguish was all fulfilled.

"Hester," said the clergyman, "farewell!"

"Shall we not meet again?" whispered she, bending her face down close to his. "Shall we not spend our immortal life together? Surely, surely, we have ransomed one another with all this wo! Thou lookest far into eternity, with those bright dying eyes! Then tell me what thou seest?"

"Hush, Hester, hush!" said he, with tremulous solemnity. "The law we broke!—the sin here so awfully revealed! — let these be in thy thoughts! I fear! I fear! It may be that, when we forgot our God—when we violated our reverence each for the other's soul—it was thenceforth vain to hope that we could meet hereafter, in an everlasting and pure reunion. God knows; and He is merciful! He hath proved His mercy, most of all, in my afflictions. By giving me this burning torture to bear upon my breast! By sending yonder dark and terrible old man, to keep the torture always at red heat! By bringing me hither to die this death of triumphant ignominy before the people! Had either of these agonies been wanting, I had been lost forever! Praised be His name! His will be done! Farewell!"

That final word came forth with the minister's expiring breath. The multitude, silent till then, broke out in a strange, deep voice of awe and wonder, which could not as yet find utterance save in this murmur that rolled so heavily after the departed spirit.

After many days, when time sufficed for the people to arrange their thoughts in reference to the foregoing scene, there was more than one account of what had been witnessed on the scaffold.

Most of the spectators testified to having seen on the breast of the unhappy minister a SCARLET LETTER—the very semblance of that worn by Hester Prynne—imprinted in the flesh. As regarded its origin, there were various explanations, all of which must necessarily have been conjectural. Some affirmed that the Reverend Mr. Dimmesdale, on the very day when Hester Prynne first wore her ignominious badge, had begun a course of penance—which he afterward, in so many futile methods, followed out—by inflicting a hideous torture on himself. Others contended that the stigma had not been produced until a long time subsequent, when old Roger Chillingworth, being a potent necromancer, had caused it to appear, through the agency of magic and poisonous drugs. Others, again—and those best able to appreciate the minister's peculiar sensibility, and the wonderful operation of his spirit upon the body—whispered their belief that the awful symbol was the effect of the ever-active tooth of remorse, gnawing from the inmost heart outwardly, and at last manifesting Heaven's dreadful judgment by the visible presence of the letter. The reader may choose among these theories. We have thrown all the light we could acquire upon the portent, and would gladly, now that it has done its office, erase its deep print out of our own brain, where long meditation has fixt it in very undesirable distinctness.

III

OF LIFE AT BROOK FARM[5]

WE had very young people with us, it is true—downy lads, rosy girls in their first teens, and children of all heights above one's knee; but these had chiefly been sent hither for education, which it was one of the objects and methods of our institution to supply. Then we had boarders from town and elsewhere, who lived with us in a familiar way, sympathized more or less in our theories, and sometimes shared in our labors.

On the whole, it was a society such as has seldom met together; nor, perhaps, could it reasonably be expected to hold together long. Persons of marked individuality—crooked sticks, as

[5] From "The Blithedale Romance," published by Houghton, Mifflin Company. Hawthorne was a member of the Brook Farm Community of Roxbury, Mass., and from it derived at least suggestions for the scene and action of this story.

some of us might be called—are not exactly the easiest to bind up into a fagot. But, so long as our union should subsist, a man of intellect and feeling, with a free nature in him, might have sought far and near without finding so many points of attraction as would allure him hitherward. We were of all creeds and opinions, and generally tolerant of all, on every imaginable subject. Our bond, it seems to me, was not affirmative, but negative. We had individually found one thing or another to quarrel with in our past life, and were pretty well agreed as to the inexpediency of lumbering along with the old system any further. As to what should be substituted there was much less unanimity. We did not greatly care—at least, I never did—for the written constitution under which our millennium had commenced. My hope was that, between theory and practise, a true and available mode of life might be struck out; and that, even should we ultimately fail, the months or years spent in the trial would not have been wasted, either as regarded passing enjoyment, or the experience which makes men wise.

Arcadians tho we were, our costume bore no resemblance to the beribboned doublets, silk breeches and stockings, and slippers fastened with artificial roses, that distinguish the pastoral people of poetry and the stage. In outward show, I humbly conceive, we looked rather like a gang of beggars, or banditti, than either a company of honest laboring-men, or a conclave of philosophers. Whatever might be our points of difference, we all of us seemed to have come to Blithedale with the one thrifty and laudable idea of wearing out our old clothes. Such garments as had an airing whenever we strode afield! Coats with high collars and with no collars, broad-skirted or swallow-tailed, and with the waist at every point between the hip and the armpit; pantaloons of a dozen successive epochs, and greatly defaced at the knees by the humiliations of the wearer before his lady-love—in short, we were a living epitome of defunct fashions, and the very raggedest presentment of men who had seen better days. It was gentility in tatters. Often retaining a scholarlike or clerical air, you might have taken us for the denizens of Grub street, intent on getting a comfortable livelihood by agricultural labor; or, Coleridge's projected Pantisocracy in full experiment; or Candide and his motley associates, at work in their cabbage-garden; or anything else that was miserably out at elbows, and most clumsily patched in the rear. We might have been sworn comrades to Falstaff's ragged regiment. Little skill as we boasted in other points of husbandry, every mother's son of us would have served admirably to stick up for a scarecrow. And the worst of the matter was that the first energetic movement essential to one downright stroke of real labor was sure to put a finish to these poor habiliments. So we gradually flung them all aside, and took to honest homespun and linsey-woolsey, as preferable, on the whole, to the plan recommended, I think, by Virgil—"*Ara nudus; sere nudus*,"—which, as Silas Foster remarked, when I translated the maxim, would be apt to astonish the women-folks.

After a reasonable training, the yeoman life

throve well with us. Our faces took the sunburn kindly; our chests gained in compass, and our shoulders in breadth and squareness; our great brown fists looked as if they had never been capable of kid gloves. The plow, the hoe, the scythe, and the hay-fork grew familiar to our grasp. The oxen responded to our voices. We could do almost as fair a day's work as Silas Foster himself, sleep dreamlessly after it, and awake at daybreak with only a little stiffness of the joints, which was usually quite gone by breakfast-time.

To be sure, our next neighbors pretended to be incredulous as to our real proficiency in the business which we had taken in hand. They told slanderous fables about our inability to yoke our own oxen, or to drive them afield when yoked, or to release the poor brutes from their conjugal bond at nightfall. They had the face to say, too, that the cows laughed at our awkwardness at milking-time, and invariably kicked over the pails; partly in consequence of our putting the stool on the wrong side, and partly because, taking offense at the whisking of their tails, we were in the habit of holding these natural fly-flappers with one hand, and milking with the other. They further averred that we hoed up whole acres of Indian corn and other crops, and drew the earth carefully about the weeds; and that we raised five hundred tufts of burdock, mistaking them for cabbages; and that, by dint of unskilful planting, few of our seeds ever came up at all, or, if they did come up, it was stern-foremost; and that we spent the better part of the month of June in reversing a field of beans, which had thrust themselves out of the ground in this unseemly way. They quoted it as nothing more than an ordinary occurrence for one or other of us to crop off two or three fingers, of a morning, by our clumsy use of the hay-cutter. Finally, and as an ultimate catastrophe, these mendacious rogues circulated a report that we communitarians were exterminated, to the last man, by severing ourselves asunder with the sweep of our own scythes!—and that the world had lost nothing by this little accident.

IV

THE DEATH OF JUDGE PYNCHEON[*]

MEANWHILE the twilight is glooming upward out of the corners of the room. The shadows of the tall furniture grow deeper, and at first become more definite; then, spreading wider, they lose their distinctness of outline in the dark gray tide of oblivion, as it were, that creeps slowly over the various objects, and the one human figure sitting in the midst of them. The gloom has not entered from without; it has brooded here all day, and now, taking its own inevitable time, will possess itself of everything. The Judge's face, indeed, rigid, and singularly white, refuses to melt into this universal solvent. Fainter and fainter grows the light. It is as if another double-handful of darkness had been scattered through the air. Now it is no longer gray, but sable. There is still a faint appearance

[*] From Chapter XVIII of "The House of the Seven Gables." Published by Houghton, Mifflin & Company.

at the window; neither a glow, nor a gleam, nor a glimmer—any phrase of light would express something far brighter than this doubtful perception, or sense, rather, that there is a window there. Has it yet vanished? No!—yes!—not quite! And there is still the swarthy whiteness —we shall venture to marry these ill-agreeing words — the swarthy whiteness of Judge Pyncheon's face. The features are all gone: there is only the paleness of them left. And how looks it now? There is no window! There is no face! An infinite, inscrutable blackness has annihilated sight! Where is our universe? All crumbled away from us; and we, adrift in chaos, may harken to the gusts of homeless wind, that go sighing and murmuring about, in quest of what was once a world!

Is there no other sound? One other, and a fearful one. It is the ticking of the Judge's watch, which, ever since Hepzibah left the room in search of Clifford, he has been holding in his hand. Be the cause what it may, this little, quiet, never-ceasing throb of Time's pulse, repeating its small strokes with such busy regularity, in Judge Pyncheon's motionless hand, has an effect of terror, which we do not find in any other accompaniment of the scene.

But, listen! That puff of the breeze was louder; it had a tone unlike the dreary and sullen one which has bemoaned itself, and afflicted all mankind with miserable sympathy, for five days past. The wind has veered about! It now comes boisterously from the northwest, and, taking hold of the aged framework of the Seven Gables, gives it a shake, like a wrestler that would try strength with his antagonist. Another and another sturdy tussle with the blast! The old house creaks again, and makes a vociferous but somewhat unintelligible bellowing in its sooty throat (the big flue, we mean, of its wide chimney), partly in complaint at the rude wind, but rather, as befits their century and a half of hostile intimacy, in tough defiance. A rumbling kind of a bluster roars behind the fireboard. A door has slammed above stairs. A window, perhaps, has been left open, or else is driven in by an unruly gust. It is not to be conceived, beforehand, what wonderful wind-instruments are these old timber mansions, and how haunted with the strangest noises, which immediately begin to sing, and sigh, and sob, and shriek—and to smite with sledge-hammers, airy but ponderous, in some distant chamber—and to tread along the entries as with stately footsteps, and rustle up and down the staircase, as with silks miraculously stiff — whenever the gale catches the house with a window open, and gets fairly into it. Would that we were not an attendant spirit here! It is too awful! This clamor of the wind through the lonely house; the Judge's quietude, as he sits invisible; and that pertinacious ticking of his watch! . . .

Yonder leaden Judge sits immovably upon our soul. Will he never stir again? We shall go mad unless he stirs! You may the better estimate his quietude by the fearlessness of a little mouse, which sits on its hind legs, in a streak of moonlight, close by Judge Pyncheon's foot, and seems to meditate a journey of exploration over this great black bulk. Ha! what has startled the nimble little mouse? It is the visage of grimalkin, outside of the window, where he appears to have posted himself for a deliberate watch. This grimalkin has a very ugly look. Is it a cat watching for a mouse, or the devil for a human soul? Would we could scare him from the window!

Thank heaven, the night is well-nigh past! The moonbeams have no longer so silvery a gleam, nor contrast so strongly with the blackness of the shadows among which they fall. They are paler, now; the shadows look gray, not black. The boisterous wind is hushed. What is the hour? Ah! the watch has at last ceased to tick; for the Judge's forgetful fingers neglected to wind it up, as usual, at ten o'clock, being half an hour or so before his ordinary bedtime—and it has run down, for the first time in five years. But the great world-clock of Time still keeps its beat. The dreary night—for, oh, how dreary seems its haunted waste, behind us—gives place to a fresh, transparent cloudless morn. Blest, blest radiance! The day-beam—even what little of it finds its way into this always dusky parlor—seems part of the universal benediction, annulling evil, and rendering all goodness possible and happiness attainable. Will Judge Pyncheon now rise up from his chair? Will he go forth, and receive the early sunbeams on his brow? Will he begin this new day—which God has smiled upon, and blest, and given to mankind—will he begin it with better purposes than the many that have been spent amiss? Or are all the deep-laid schemes of yesterday as stubborn in his heart, and as busy in his brain, as ever? . . .

The morning sunshine glimmers through the

foliage, and, beautiful and holy as it is, shuns not to kindle up your face. Rise up, thou subtle, worldly, selfish, iron-hearted hypocrite, and make thy choice whether still to be subtle, worldly, selfish, iron-hearted, and hypocritical, or to tear these sins out of thy nature, tho they bring the life-blood with them! The Avenger is upon thee! Rise up, before it be too late!

What! Thou art not stirred by this last appeal? No, not a jot! And there we see a fly—one of your common house-flies, such as are always buzzing on the window-pane—which has smelt out Governor Pyncheon, and alights, now on his forehead, now on his chin, and now, heaven help us! is creeping over the bridge of his nose, toward the would-be chief magistrate's wide-open eyes! Canst thou not brush the fly away? Art thou too sluggish? Thou man, that hadst so many busy projects yesterday! Art thou too weak, that wast so powerful? Not brush away a fly? Nay, then, we give thee up!

And hark! the shop-bell rings. After hours like these latter ones, through which we have borne our heavy tale, it is good to be made sensible that there is a living world, and that even this old, lonely mansion retains some manner of connection with it. We breathe more freely, emerging from Judge Pyncheon's presence into the street before the Seven Gables.

END OF VOLUME IX